PARIS FRANCE

Books by Gertrude Stein in Liveright Paperback Editions

JUAN GRIS   *Roses (1912)*

PARIS FRANCE

By
GERTRUDE STEIN

LIVERIGHT

NEW YORK

*First published in 1940. This current edition
is published by permission of the estate and/or heirs
of Gertrude Stein.*

LIVERIGHT PAPERBOUND EDITION 1970

MANUFACTURED IN THE UNITED STATES OF AMERICA

Liveright Publishing Corporation, 500 Fifth Avenue,
New York, N.Y. 10110

W. W. Norton & Company Ltd., 37 Great Russell Street, London WC1B 3NU

ISBN 0-87140-231-9

1 2 3 4 5 6 7 8 9

The publishers wish to thank the artists who have allowed their paintings or drawings to be used as illustrations to " Paris France." They are particularly grateful to Monsieur Henry Kahnweiler, of the Galérie Simon, Paris, for his help in arranging for the reproduction of most of the subjects.

LIST OF ILLUSTRATIONS

vii

PART I

PARIS, FRANCE IS exciting and peaceful.

I was only four years old when I was first in Paris and talked french there and was photographed there and went to school there, and ate soup for early breakfast and had leg of mutton and spinach for lunch, I always liked spinach, and a black cat jumped on my mother's back. That was more exciting than peaceful. I do not mind cats but I do not like them to jump on my back. There are lots of cats in Paris and in France and they can do what they like, sit on the vegetables or among the groceries, stay in or go out. It is extraordinary that they fight so little among themselves considering how many cats there are. There are two things that french animals do not do, cats do not fight much and do not howl much and chickens do not get flustered running across the road, if they start to cross the road they keep on going which is what french people do too.

Anybody driving a car in Paris must know that. Anybody leaving the sidewalk to go on or walking anywhere goes on at a certain pace and that pace keeps up and nothing startles them nothing frightens them nothing makes them go faster or slower nothing not the most violent or unexpected noise makes them jump, or change their pace or their direction. If anybody jumps back or jumps at all in the streets of Paris you can be sure they are foreign not french. That is peaceful and exciting.

So I was in Paris a year when I was four to five and then I was back in America. A child does not forget but other things happen.

A little later in San Francisco there was more french.

After all everybody, that is, everybody who writes is interested in living inside themselves in order to tell what is inside themselves. That is why writers have to have two countries, the one where they belong and the one in which they live really. The second one is romantic, it is separate from themselves, it is not real but it is really there.

The English Victorians were like that about Italy, the early nineteenth century Americans were like that about Spain, the middle nineteenth century Americans were like that about England, my generation the end of the nineteenth century American generation was like that about France.

Of course sometimes people discover their own country as if it were the other, a recent instance of that is Louis Bromfield discovering America, there have been a few English like that too, Kipling for instance discovered England but in general that other country that you need to be free in is the other country not the country where you really belong.

In San Francisco it was easy that it should be France. Of course it might have been Spain or China, but really in San Francisco as a child one really knew too much about Spain and China, and France was interesting while Spain and China were familiar, and daily. France was not daily it just came up again and again.

It came up first in such different books, Jules Verne and Alfred de Vigny and it came up in my mother's clothes and the gloves and the sealskin caps and muffs and the boxes they came in.

There was the smell of Paris in that.

And then for quite a long while it was very easy to forget France.

The next thing I remember about France were the Henry Henrys and Sarah Bernhardt, the Panorama of the Battle of Waterloo and Millet's Man With The Hoe.

The Panorama of the Battle of Waterloo.

One of the pleasantest things those of us who write or paint do is to have the daily miracle. It does come.

I was about eight years old and it came with the Panorama of the Battle of Waterloo.

It was painted by a frenchman, I wonder if it would not be interesting to have one now, one of those huge panoramas, where you stood in the center on a platform and all around you on every side of you was an oil painting.   You were completely surrounded by an oil painting.

It was then I first realised the difference between a painting and out of doors.   I realised that a painting is always a flat surface and out of doors never is, and that out of doors is made up of air and a painting has no air, the air is replaced by a flat surface, and anything in a painting that imitates air is illustration and not art.   I seem to have felt all that very intensely standing on the platform and being all surrounded by an oil painting.

And then there was Sarah Bernhardt.

San Francisco had lots of french people in it, and a french theatre and one naturally knew little girls and boys who talked french at home quite naturally. And so when a french actor or actress came to San Francisco they always stayed a long time.

They liked it there and of course when actresses or actors stay anywhere they always act, so naturally there was a great deal of French spoken in the theatre.

4

It was then that I found out quite naturally, that french is a spoken language and English a written one.

In France whenever anybody writes anything and wants anybody to know what it is like they read it out loud. If it is in English it is natural to pass the manuscript to them and let them read it but if it is in french it is natural to read it out loud.

French is a spoken language English really is not.

Sarah Bernhardt made me see the thin arms of frenchwomen. When I came to Paris and saw the little midinettes and Montmartoises they all had them. It was only many years later when the styles changed, in those days they wore long skirts, that I realised what sturdy legs went with those thin arms. That is what makes the french such good soldiers the sturdy legs, thin arms and sturdy legs, if you see what I mean, peaceful and exciting.

That is what makes all the french able to ride up hill on bicycles the way they do, no hill is so steep but that slowly pedalling up and up they go, men and girls and little children, the sturdy legs and thin arms.

The other thing that was french there in San Francisco were the family of Henry Henrys. That was their name.

There was a father and mother they were known as

Monsieur and Madame Henry and there were five children the oldest Henry Henry played the violin We used to go there in the afternoon and stay to dinner and then we used to dance the Henry children and ourselves, to the french music of the violin.

And we always for dinner had a roast of mutton, a gigot they called it, cooked the same way as when I went to school in Paris and potatoes in the butter around it, clean looking potatoes, not so dark as when they were cooked American. But the thing that was most exciting were the knives and forks. The knives had been sharpened so much that the blade was as thin as a dagger with a slight bend on top and the forks so light that when you pressed on them they bent. These knives and forks were the most passionately french things I knew, I might say I ever knew.

Then there was Millet's Man With The Hoe.

I had never really wanted a photograph of a picture before I saw Millet's Man With The Hoe. I was about twelve or thirteen years old, I had read Eugenie Grandet of Balzac, and I did have some feeling about what french country was like but The Man With The Hoe made it different, it made it ground not country, and France has been that to me ever since. France is made of ground, of earth.

When I managed to get a photograph of the picture and took it home my eldest brother looked at it and said what is it and I said it is Millet's Man With The Hoe. It is a hell of a hoe said my eldest brother.

But that is the way french country is, it is ground like that and they work at it just that way with just that kind of a hoe.

All this was all the Paris France I really knew then and then for a very long time I forgot about Paris and about France.

Then one day when I was at college at Radcliffe in Cambridge Massachusetts, I was on a train and sitting next to me was a frenchman. I recognised him as a visiting lecturer and I spoke to him. We talked about American college women. Very wonderful he said and very interesting but and he looked at me earnestly, really not one of them, now you must admit that, not one of them could feel with Alfred de Musset that le seul bien qui me reste au monde c'est d'avoir quelque fois pleuré. I was young then but I knew what he meant that they would not feel like that. That and a certain interest in Zola as a realist but not as much interest as in the Russian realists was all that Paris meant to me until after the medical school when I settled down in Paris France.

PART II

ALICE TOKLAS SAID, my grandmother's cousin's wife told me that her daughter had married the son of the engineer who had built the Eiffel Tower and his name was not Eiffel.

When we were having a book printed in France we complained about the bad alignment. Ah they explained that is because they use machines now, machines are bound to be inaccurate, they have not the intelligence of human beings, naturally the human mind corrects the faults of the hand but a machine of course there are errors. The reason why all of us naturally began to live in France is because France has scientific methods, machines and electricity, but does not really believe that these things have anything to do with the real business of living. Life is tradition and human nature.

And so in the beginning of the twentieth century when a new way had to be found naturally they needed France.

Really not, french people really do not believe that anything is important except daily living and the

LASCAUX

Le Sacré Coeur

ground that gives it to them and defending themselves from the enemy. Government has no importance except insofar as it does that.

I remember so well it was during the 1914 war and they were all french and they were talking about women voting and one of the women who was listening said, oh dear I have to stand in line for so many things coal and sugar and candles and meat and now to vote, oh dear.

After all it does not make any difference and they know it does not make any difference.

When I was first in Paris and for many years I had a servant, we were very good friends her name was Hélène. One day quite accidentally, I do not know how it happened because I was not at all interested, I said to her, Hélène what political party does your husband belong to. She always had told me everything even the most intimate troubles with her family and her husband but when I said that, what party does your husband belong to, her face grew rigid. She did not answer. What is the matter with you Hélène I said, is it a secret. No Mademoiselle she answered it is not a secret but one does not tell it. One does not tell the political party one belongs to. Even I have a political party but I do not tell it.

I had been in France many years but I was surprised and I began to ask around and they were all
like that. They all had that same expression of, it is
not a secret but one does not tell it. A son did not
know what party his father belonged to nor the
father the son's.

It is because of this that the recent front commun
had such a short life. They told, they all had to tell
and to tell all day long, what their political party was
and so of course it could not last long. It just could
not.

No, publicity in France is really not important,
tradition and their private life and the soil which
always produces something, that is what counts.

Mrs. Lindberg was in Paris and she and I were
talking. In America of course she had suffered they
had suffered from publicity. In England they had
payed no attention to them but they the Lindbergs
knew and England knew that they were there. In
France they pay attention to you when you meet,
but they do not bother you because in between they
do not know that you are there.

When Fania Marinoff came to Paris she said she
would like to meet so and so. Sorry I said I do not
know them. But you know who they are, oh yes,
I said, vaguely. Then she mentioned others. Some

I knew and some I did not. She could not understand, in New York, she said, if I knew you I would know them. Yes yes I said but not in Paris. Not to know the well known in Paris does not argue yourself unknown, because nobody knows anybody whom they do not know.

Now for some if not for all these reasons, Paris was where the twentieth century was.

It was important too that Paris was where fashions were made. To be sure there were moments when they seemed to dress better in Barcelona and in New York but not really.

It was in Paris that the fashions were made, and it is always in the great moments when everything changes that fashions are important, because they make something go up in the air or go down or go around that has nothing to do with anything.

Fashion is the real thing in abstraction. The one thing that has no practical side to it and so quite naturally Paris which has always made fashions was where everybody went in 1900. They needed the background of tradition of profound conviction that men and women and children do not change, that science is interesting but does not change anything, that democracy is real but that governments unless they tax you too much or get you defeated by the enemy are of no importance, that is the background that everybody needed in 1900.

It is funny about art and literature, fashions being part of it. Two years ago everybody was saying that France was down and out, was sinking to be a second-rate power, etcetera etcetera. And I said but I do not think so because not for years not since the war have hats been as various and lovely and as french as they are now. Not only are they to be found in the good shops but everywhere there is a real milliner there is a pretty french little hat.

I do not believe that when the characteristic art and literature of a country is active and fresh I do not think that country is in its decline. There is no pulse so sure of the state of a nation as its characteristic art product which has nothing to do with its material life. And so when hats in Paris are lovely and french and everywhere then France is alright.

So Paris was the place that suited those of us that were to create the twentieth century art and literature, naturally enough.

So many things. They change occupations so easily, they are very conservative very traditional and they change occupations easily. They may start as bakers and then they become agent for an estate and then they become a banker all one man and all in ten years and then they retire.

It is also amusing that it always takes about seven men to do anything, to build a whole road or to put up three telegraph poles or to build a fair or to take down one tree. It does not make any difference seven men, thereabout, are always there at it, it takes several to talk several to look on and one or two to work, so whatever there is to do it always takes about the same number. Now this was very important because once again this made a background of unreality which was very necessary for anybody having to create the twentieth century. The nineteenth century knew just what to do with each man but the twentieth century inevitably was not to know and so Paris was the place to be.

And then the way they feel about the dead, it is so friendly so simply friendly and though inevitable not a sadness and though occurring not a shock. There is no difference between death and life in France and that too made it inevitable that they were the background of the twentieth century.

Naturally it was foreigners who did it there in France because all these things being french it made it be their tradition and it being a tradition it was not the twentieth century.

There are always so many foreigners everywhere but particularly in France.

One day Gerald Berners and I were walking and he suggested that it would make a nice book to put in it all the aphorisms which were not true.

We thought of a great many and among them, familiarity breeds contempt and no man is a hero to his valet. We concluded that in fully ninety per cent of the cases it was the other way.

Familiarity does not breed contempt. On the contrary the more familiar it is the more rare and beautiful it is. Take the quarter in which one lives, it is lovely, it is a place rare and beautiful and to leave it is awful.

I remember once hearing a conversation on the street in Paris and it ended up, and so there it was there was nothing for them to do, they had to leave the quarter. There it was, there was nothing else to do they had to leave the most wonderful place in the world, wonderful because it was there where they had always lived.

Paris quarters were like that, we all had our quarters, to be sure when later we left them and went back to them they did look dreary, not at all like the lovely quarter in which we are living now. So familiarity did not breed contempt.

And then not being a hero to one's valet. Is there anybody in the world even yourself who is as pleased with your publicity as your servant certainly your french servant is pleased there is no doubt about that, past present and future servants all of them are pleased with that.

So then which quarters of Paris were important and when.

From 1900 to 1930, Paris did change a lot. They always told me that America changed but it really did not change as much as Paris did in those years that is the Paris that one can see, but then there is no remembering what it looked like before and even no remembering what it looks like now.

We none of us lived in old parts of Paris then. We lived in the rue de Fleurus just a hundred year old quarter, a great many of us lived around there and on the boulevard Raspail which was not even cut through then and when it was cut through all the rats and animals came underneath our house and we had to have one of the vermin catchers of Paris come and clean us out, I wonder if they exist any more now, they have disappeared along with the horses and enormous wagons that used to clean out the sewers under the houses that were not in the new sewerage system, now even the oldest houses are in the new system. It is nice in France they adapt themselves to everything slowly they change completely but all the time they know that they are as they were.

Belley the little country town now even all summer long eats grape fruits, they have concluded that grape fruits are a necessary luxury.

Our old servant Hélène who was with us before the war for many years, learned from us that children should be raised differently and more hygienically and raise it in that way she did but all the same one day I heard her talking to her six year old little boy and saying you are a good little boy, yes mother he said, and you love your mother very much, yes mother he said, and you will grow up loving your mother she said, yes mother he said and then she said you will be grown up and you will leave me for a woman will you not, yes mother he said.

I always remember too when the Titanic went down and everybody was so moved at the heroism and the saving of women and children, I do not see anything sensible in that, said Hélène, what use are women and children alone in the world, what kind of life can they lead, it would have been lots more sensible, said Hélène, if they had drawn lots and saved a certain number of complete families much more sensible, said Hélène.

PICASSO   *Café Interior* (*1901*)

And that is what made Paris and France the natural background of the art and literature of the twentieth century. Their tradition kept them from changing and yet they naturally saw things as they were, and accepted life as it is, and mixed things up without any reason at the same time. Foreigners were not romantic to them, they were just facts, nothing was sentimental they were just there, and strangely enough it did not make them make the art and literature of the twentieth century but it made them be the inevitable background for it.

So from 1900 to 1930 those of us who lived in Paris did not live in picturesque quarters even those who lived in Montmartre like Picasso and Bracque did not live in old houses, they lived in fifty year old houses at most and now we all live in the ancient quarter near the river, now that the twentieth century is decided and has its character we all tend to want to live in seventeenth century houses, not barracks of ateliers as we did then. The seventeenth century houses are just as cheap as our barracks of ateliers were then but now we need the picturesque the splendid we need the air and space you only get in old quarters. It was Picasso who said the other day when they were talking about tearing down the insalubrious parts of Paris but it is only in the insalubrious quarters that there is sun and air and space, and it is true, and we are all living there the beginners and the middle ones and the older ones and the old ones we all live in old houses in ramshackle quarters. Well all this is natural enough.

Familiarity does not breed contempt, anything one does every day is important and imposing and anywhere one lives is interesting and beautiful. And that is all as it should be.

So it begins to be reasonable that the twentieth century whose mechanics, whose crimes, whose standardisation began in America, needed the background of Paris, the place where tradition was so firm that they could look modern without being different, and where their acceptance of reality is so great that they could let any one have the emotion of unreality.

Then there is their feeling about foreigners that helps a lot.

After all to the french the difference between being a foreigner and being an inhabitant is not very serious. There are so many foreigners and all who are real to them are those that inhabit Paris and France. In that they are different from other people. Other people find foreigners more real to them when they are in their own country but to the french foreigners are only real to them when they are in France.

Naturally they come to France. What is more natural for them to do than that.

I remember an old servant invented a nice name for foreigners, there were Americans they existed because she was our servant and we were there, and then there was something she called a creole ecossais, we never did find out where that came from.

Of course they all came to France a great many to paint pictures and naturally they could not do that at home, or write they could not do that at home either, they could be dentists at home she knew all about that even before the war, Americans were a practical people and dentistry was practical. To be sure certainly, she was the most practical, because when her little boy was ill, of course she was awfully unhappy because it was her little boy but then also it was all to do over again because she did have to have one child, any french person has to have one child, and now after two years it was all to do again money and everything. And still why not of course why not.

So all this simple clarity in respect to seeing life as it is, the animal and social life in human beings as it is, the money value of human and social and animal life as it is, without brutality or without simplicity, what is it to-day a french woman said to me about an American writer, it is false without being artificial.

It did not take the twentieth century to make them say that as it has taken the twentieth century to make other people say that.

Foreigners belong in France because they have always been here and did what they had to do there and remained foreigners there. Foreigners should be foreigners and it is nice that foreigners are foreigners and that they inevitably are in Paris and in France.

They are beginning now at last, cinemas and the world war have slowly made them realise, what nationality the foreigners are. In a little hotel where we stayed some time they spoke of us as English, no we said no we are Americans, at last one of them a little annoyed at our persistance said but it is all the same. Yes I answered like the french and Italians all the same. Well before the war they could not have said that nor felt the unpleasantness of the answer. Then we had a Finnish maid here in the country, and once she came in all beaming, it is wonderful, she said, the milk woman knows Finland, she knows where Finland is, she knows all about Finland, why, said the Finnish maid, I have known very educated people who did not know where

Finland was but she knew. Well did she know. No but she did have the ancient tradition of french politeness and that was that. They do, of course.

But really what they do do is to respect art and letters, if you are a writer you have privileges, if you are a painter you have privileges and it is pleasant having those privileges. I always remember coming in from the country to my garage where I usually kept my car and the garage was full more than full, it was the moment of the automobile salon, but said I what can I do, well said the man in charge I'll see and then he came back and said in a low voice, there is a corner and in this corner I have put the car of Monsieur the academician and next to it I will put yours the others can stay outside and it is quite true even in a garage an academician and a woman of letters takes precedence even of millionaires or politicians, they do, it is quite incredible but they do, the police treat artists and writers respectfully too, well that too is intelligent on the part of France and unsentimental, because after all the way everything is remembered is by the writers and painters of the period, nobody really lives who has not been well written about and in realising that the french show their usual sense of reality and a belief in a sense of reality is the twentieth century, people may not have it but they do believe in it.

They are funny even now they are funny, all the peasants of the village, well not all but a number of them were eating their bread and wine, they do quite nicely now have jam on their bread, nice jam made of a mixture of apricots and apples, just how they happen at the same time I do not quite know, yes perhaps late apricots and early apples, it is very good.

So we were talking and they said to me, now tell me, why does the french chamber vote itself two more years of existence, and we, well of course we never do have anything to say but why do they, tell us. Well I said why not, you know it they know it, and beside if they are there why should not they stay there. Well said they laughing let's be like Spain. Let's have a civil war. Well said I what is the use, after all, after all their shooting each other up they are going to have their king again any way the king's son. Then for a change said they, why do not we have the king's nephew.

That is the way they feel about it, the only thing that is important is the daily life, and so the gangsters, so the twentieth century had really nothing to teach the french countryman therefore it was the proper background for the art and literature of the twentieth century.

The impressionists.

The twentieth century did not invent but it made a great fuss about series production, series production really began in the nineteenth century, that is natural enough, machines are bound to make series production.

So although there was more fuss made about machines and series production in the twentieth century than in the nineteenth of course it was a nineteenth century thing.

The impressionists and they were nineteenth century had as their aspiration and their ideal one painting a day, really two paintings a day, the morning painting and the afternoon painting actually it might have been the early morning and the early afternoon and the late afternoon. But after all there is a limit to the human hand after all painting is hand painting so actually even at their most excited moment they rarely did more than two more frequently one, and very often not one a day, most generally not one a day. They had the dream of a series production but as Monsieur Darantiere said about printing after all they had not the faults or the qualities of machines.

So Paris was the natural background for the twentieth century, America knew it too well, knew the twentieth century too well to create it, for America there was a glamour in the twentieth century that made it not be material for creative activity. England was consciously refusing the twentieth century, knowing full well that they had gloriously created the nineteenth century and perhaps the twentieth century was going to be too many for them, so they were quite self consciously denying the twentieth century but France was not worrying about it, what is was and what was is, was their point of view of which they were not very conscious, they were too occupied with their daily life to worry about it, beside the last half of the nineteenth century had really not interested them very much, not since the end of the romantic movement, they had worked hard, they always work hard, but the last half of the nineteenth century had really not interested them very much. As the peasants always say every year comes to an end, and they like it when the bad weather does not keep them from working, they like to work, it is a pastime for them work is, and so although the last half of the nineteenth century did not interest them they did work. And now the twentieth century had come and it might be more interesting, if it was to be really interesting of course they would not work quite so much, being interested does sometimes stop one from working, work might then be even somewhat disturbing and distracting. So the twentieth century had come it began with 1901.

PART III

A N A M E R I C A N W H O had read as far as this as far as it had been written said to me, but you do not mention the relation of french men to french men, of french men to french women of french women to french women of french women to french children of french men to french children of french children to french children. No I have not and for a very simple reason, there is no relation between them, all the contact between them all is so fixed and inevitable, so definite and so real that there is no question of either nature nor choice nor mistake. There can be no mistake and they cannot be mistaken.

Once in talking to the Baronne Pierlot a very old french friend she said about something when I said but Madame Pierlot it is natural, no said Madame Pierlot it may be nature but it is not natural. She is eighty-six and her granddaughter eight and it is difficult at times to know whether they are both eighty-six or whether they are both eight.

I once wrote and said what is the use of being a boy if you are to grow up to be a man what is the use and what is the use. But in France a boy is a man of his age the age he is and so there is no question of a boy growing up to be a man and what is the use, because at every stage of being alive he is completely a man alive at that time.

This accounts for the very curious relation of every french man to his mother. Just as he is always alive all the time and every moment of the time as a man so he is all his life continually a son dependent upon his mother. There is no break in that dependence even if a man is sixty years old and that in France very often does happen, the man is always dependent upon his mother, and so a frenchman is always a man because there is nothing inevitably different between being a boy and a man in a frenchman's life and he is always a son because he is always dependent upon his mother for his strength his morality, his hope and his despair, his future and his past. A frenchman always goes completely to pieces when his mother dies, he is fortunate if another woman has come into his life who is a mother to him.

And now it is once more an August and September and there is once more a crisis and once more the farmers the gentle farmers talk about life as it is. One of the gentlest said to me the other day. We used to think not we but everybody used to think that it was kings who were ambitious who were greedy and who brought misery to the people who had no way to resist them. But now well democracy has shown us that what is evil are the grosses têtes, the big heads, all big heads are greedy for money and power, they are ambitious that is the reason they are big heads and so they are at the head of the government and the result is misery for the people. They talk about cutting off the heads of the grosses têtes but now we know that there will be other grosses têtes and they will be all the same.

He shook his head sadly and went back to his harvesting.

And so there is no use going on except that the summers follow one after the other and the fashions go with the seasons.

If you like fashions you get tired of crises, and the french like fashions they do not like them they naturally create them and crises are occasionally a help to fashions, an occasional crisis is, but not many of them, many crises in succession interfere with fashions and so a workman said to me yesterday, We have had enough of what they make us do we are tired of crises. And he was right, the season and the fashions that exist with the seasons are the things

France lives by, the earth has its seasons and the people who live on that earth have fashions and that is all.

Fashions are so natural, we were all together at a house here in the country and somebody said something of Madame Pierlot's father, what was he. Ah was the answer, Madame Pierlot is eighty-six and so all who are younger have naturally forgotten about her father, but oh some one answered, when we go up to the attic and find clothes in which to dress up we always find a piece of ermine and on this ermine is written the name of Madame Pierlot's father. What kind of ermine asked some one, and the ermine was described, ah yes was the answer in that case he was the judge of the Cour d'appel. There are fashions that change and fashions that do not change or fashions that change slowly but there are always fashions. But fashions as the workman said cannot live while there are interferences from the outside, an occasional crisis is alright but not many of them.

It is because of this that the American married to a frenchwoman remarked my American sister rises wonderfully to a crisis but my french wife sees to it that a crisis does not arise.

There is also another matter, once long ago there

had been a summer rumor of earthquakes and a servant of a friend of ours living in the avenue Victor Hugo said we must have an earthquake in Paris very soon, but why said my friend indignantly, ah because Madame of course we must suivre le mouvement, follow the fashion.

But the thing to remember is that the french know the difference between a fashion and something that is being done that is not a fashion, some people follow everything but the french have a delicate sense, they know what is a fashion and what is not a fashion, and just following the way some nations do is not following a fashion, and of course they do not want to feel any sense of obligation or obedience, obligation and obedience is the death of fashion and therefore as the workman said we have had enough of what they make us do.

And so all this may be only a fire drill, by all this I mean war and thought of war, the french say if you can remember three generations of war it is enough, you remember your father, he ate horses' heads in the war of '70, you remember your husband he was killed in '17, and your brother who was prisoner in Switzerland and it cost a good deal of money and your son and he is now home on leave and he was called away before his leave was over by a telegram to go back to his regiment and now, a thing like this including a daughter who was a school teacher and had only been married five months and was called back to evacuate the school children, all this was enough to make any one's head go right away.

But after all it might only be a fire drill, it might only be a make believe, any frenchman knows that you really ought not to know the difference between danger and no danger.

I was on the boat once going to America. Abbé Dimnet was there too and they talked about a fire drill, they had one, everybody was supposed to put on safety belts and a boat was lowered but nobody got into the boat, Abbé Dimnet was indignant, he said to me they should get into the boat, tell the captain, said I, I will, said he, he came back, what did the captain say I asked, he said, said he furious, he said that you could not get into the boat unless the ship was stopped it would be too dangerous and to stop the ship was too costly and took too much time. The Abbé Dimnet was furious he said yes that is the way it is they prepare they prepare and they never know whether they can do what they are prepared for.

The french are polite, they naturally are, they never believe in having a surprise inspection, they always believe in announcing it beforehand, so that everything can be ready to be inspected and so that no one will have any unpleasant feelings, and why not, it is always pleasanter to be polite and as the french are completely frank, they really cannot lie, if you let any plumber anybody talk long enough they will always tell the truth. They have so completely the sense of reality that they cannot really lie, they cannot really eventually not tell the facts as they are, and therefore they can be as polite as they want at any time, because politeness does not interfere with facts, politeness is just another fact.

We once had a chimney-fire and so we decided to heat by electricity. We had had several chimney-fires and we had had enough of them and it was in the winter and we wanted the new system put in quickly. A frenchman who came to talk about it said he would but not very quickly, but you must do it quickly we said but he said that he would do his best but it would not be as quickly as we thought it would be done, finally he said alright it would be done quickly, you see he said reflectively it is atavism, your being ladies and your asking me to do it quickly, I cannot help myself I must do what you ask, it is, said he, with a helpless smile, it is atavism. And it was and he did it very quickly indeed.

Ah yes the village is sad, the men are all gone and one of the women passing said ah yes and now once again it is evening, well yes once again it is it is evening.

And so France cannot change it can always have its fashions but it cannot change. And this brings me to dogs.

The french dogs which are native are useful dogs beautiful dogs but dogs that work. They are shepherd dogs and hunting dogs.

It is funny about dogs. Dogs resemble the nation which creates them at least we suppose so. Dogs are certainly like the people that own them and have them with them all the time. I like the word pastime as the french use it, it sounds so like the English word and yet the french make it so completely their own, who had it first this I do not know, but they certainly use it perhaps best. Dogs which are not useful dogs are a pastime, as one woman once said to me, one has a great deal of pleasure out of dogs because one can spoil them as one cannot spoil one's children. If the children are spoiled, one's future is spoilt but dogs one can spoil without any thought of the future and that is a great pleasure.

So the french dogs which are useful are native, the various shepherd dogs and the various hunting dogs, they are beautiful and they are useful, they are companions but they are not pets, they cannot be spoiled with pleasure to the spoiler as dogs that are pets can be spoiled, beside the useful animal is never a thing which is in or out of fashion, I always like the story of the shepherd near Aix-en-Provence, he was taking his dog to kill him he used to kill them by hanging, when they are eight years old they no longer interested themselves in sheep, and as bread is dear you cannot keep a dog who is not interested in his trade. They know that at eight years of age he will stop being interested in tending sheep and so with tears streaming from his eyes off he goes to hang him. There is another nice story of a dog in Aix-en-Provence, there was a girl in a café who was very fond of a dog who used to come there regularly with a man and she regularly gave him a lump of sugar, one day the man came in without the dog and said the dog was dead. The girl had the lump of sugar in her hand and when she heard the dog was dead tears came to her eyes and she ate the lump of sugar.

The french have to have as pet dogs foreign ones which they change and fashion in their own way, and the mode in these dogs changes, they mostly always come back again, as long as I have known

France first it was poodles then it was Belgian griffons, fox-terriers, always called a fox, when I first heard it called a fox I thought it was a fox until I saw it, then Alsatian wolf hounds and Pekinese and then wire-haired terriers and now poodles, they having invented a new way to shave the poodle and a new color to make the poodles, so they are in again and this time at the same time the fox terriers have come back. Now all these dogs being of no use can be made fashionable, because fashion must never be useful, must very often be exotic, and must always be made to be french. That is what fashion is and it must change.

And this brings me back once more to the question of the resemblance of a dog to its country people.

It is a puzzle why are german dogs all rather timid gentle friendly and obedient, they are that, the characteristic german dogs, it kind of cheers one up that some time they the people will be that because people and dogs must be alike in a country in which they are born and bred and have descended. There are the poodles, the dachshunds, even the dog which is a kind of a bull, the Bismark dog is gentle and the german black police-dog is a much gentler animal than the Alsatian wolf hound, it is a funny thing this, being fond of poodles, and always having them I bother about all this. I thought poodles were french but the french breed always has to be refreshed by the german one, and the german pincher is so much more gentle than our Chichuachua little dog which it resembles, and so everything would be a puzzle if it were not certain that logic is right, and is stronger than the will of man. We will see.

The characteristic art product of a country is the pulse of the country, France did produce better hats and fashions than ever these last two years and is therefore very alive and Germany's music and musicians have been dead and gone these last two years and so Germany is dead well we will see, it is so, of course as all these things are necessarily true.

The fancy and imagination of every country is so different. I have just written a child's book called The World Is Round and an English friend who lives in France here being married to a Frenchman, Betty Leyris, has a three months old baby, and I said I would give her a copy for little Johnny when he could read. And said Betty I hope by the time he is old enough to read it that the world will still be round.

Now that is purely an English imagination that and so each country is important at different times because the world in general needs a different imagination at different times and so there is the Paris France from 1900 to 1939, where everybody had to be to be free.

The war is going on this war and we were all waiting and the telephone rang, well and it was the Mère Mollard announcing that her quenelles had turned on her, she had ice and she had put them on ice and she had taken them out to look at them and they had turned sour. Well anyway even if there is no food and there is a war and she is not a good cook cooking is important.

The Doctor Chaboux managed well he did not try but he did kill a hare with his automobile on the road and we were invited to eat it, with jugged hare you always have to eat boiled potatoes and really boiled potatoes and hare were very good. They say in the country here that potatoes are the healthiest of all foods, to be sure they do eat a great deal of bread as well and wine but after all, they say, you do give potatoes to sick people you do not give them bread, bread is for the strong, potatoes are for the healthy and the ill, but what really is important is that in this very country where the twentieth century was to be found and celebrated in the arts they still call them the Mère Mollard, or the Père Mollard or the Fils Mollard and they call a painter who is old cher maitre. They will do that. I cannot write too much upon how necessary it is to be completely conservative that is particularly traditional in order to be free. And so France is and was. Sometimes it is important and sometimes it is not, but from 1900 to 1939, it certainly was.

War is more like a novel than it is like real life and that is its eternal fascination. It is a thing based on reality but invented, it is a dream made real, all the things that make a novel but not really life.

And that makes one think a great deal about music, war naturally does make music but certainly this war with everybody really everybody listening to the radio, there is nothing but music. There used to be a song that was sung called Music In The Air, but when that song was written nobody really thought that there would be all this music in the air.

After all really civilised countries do not continuously make music, and that is the reason that France and England are the most civilised countries. They are not everlastingly making music.

And therefore France was so important in the period between 1900 and 1939, it was a period when there really was a serious effort made by humanity to be civilised, the world was round and there really were not left any unknown on it and so everybody decided to be civilised. England had the disadvantage of believing in progress, and progress has really nothing to do with civilisation, but France could be civilised without having progress on her mind, she could believe in civilisation in and for itself, and so she was the natural background for this period.

The relation of men to women and men to men and women to women in a state of being civilised has to be very much considered. Frenchmen love older women, that is women who have already done more living, and that has something to do with civilisation, they do not believe in comradeship really not with any one, they said in their revolution Egalité Fraternité Liberté, but these qualities should be left to war and politics, they are not human. Humanly speaking, Frenchwomen nor Frenchmen do not really interest themselves in intimacy, intimacy is something essentially uncivilised, civilisation makes young men interested in a woman of thirty and an interest in a spirit of equality with a very young woman is more or less a sign of senility, and senility is of course not civilised.

A soldier at the front from this village wrote a letter, he was seeing the evacuation of the German villages and he writes, it is sad to see farms evacuated, to see animals leaving the places they are used to, it is very sad, you my father and I, we understand this thing but my mother she will not understand.

Well that is one way of feeling and we had made a sudden visit to Paris and were back here in the hills far away, and one of the farmers, he is a tall bearded farmer who drinks a great deal of wine, but is for all that a most excellent farmer, he asked me what the people in Paris were doing. They were all carrying gas masks, I answered, ah yes he said, pour remplacer les muguets to replace lilies of the valley as a decoration.

A farmer naturally says such things in France but he is not intimate, he is not intimate with man, woman or child or animal, he is not intimate, it is not civilised to be intimate and the French need to be civilised and in order to do so he must have tradition and freedom and with tradition and freedom one cannot be intimate with any one.

This too was very necessary in this twentieth century, when the present was so completely dominating.

The only thing any Frenchman minds in war is sleeping on straw, nobody sleeps on straw, no French vagabond no French soldier, they must have a roof over them and something that is built like a bed. The only thing any French soldier ever complains about is when that awful thing happens to him, he has to sleep on straw. Once more, it is not the discomfort, it is the destruction of civilisation that he resents, and he is right.

Otherwise war is full of fashion and Frenchmen although they want peace, realise the quality of fashion profoundly inherent in war.

A woman in the village, that was before this war began said to me one day, they used to laugh gayly before the war she meant 1914 war and since then they have not laughed, they seem to enjoy themselves but they do not laugh, she wondered was it that they had forgotten or that you did not laugh, perhaps she said if there is a whole generation that never heard of war they will laugh. Perhaps not, she said, she realised that it might never again happen that any one would really laugh.

Fashion is in everything except in the making of war, but war makes fashions.

Back again to 1900 when there were fashions but no war.

Well not exactly because there was a war, there is always mostly always a war somewhere but not a general European war.

It is hard to believe that there is always going to be a general European war and yet well yet it does make something that there always is going to be a general European war, it makes logic.

I was in the country here in France last September the September when there was not a war. I live in the French country in the summer in a little village where there are perhaps twenty families and I know them all and their oxen and cows and dogs, I know them all and they know me and my car and my dogs. Well it was that September when there was no war and I felt as we all did and I went out on the road walking with my dogs, and I had just heard that one of my neighbours Monsieur Lambert had been mobilised as they were all mobilised because there might be going to be a war. He is a tall thin man, a gentle soul, a good farmer and a good soldier, forty-five years old. I met him with his wife and oxen. And I said you are leaving to go, Monsieur Lambert. Yes, he said, and my wife is crying. Is there going to be a war, I said. No, he said, my wife is crying but there is not going to be a war. Why not, I said. Because, said he, it is not logical. You see I am forty-five years old, I fought the whole of the last war, my son is seventeen years old, he and I would fight this war. It is not logical mademoiselle that I at forty-five who fought the war, with a son of seventeen, should believe in a general European war.

It is not logical. Now said he, if I were sixty and my grandson was seventeen, we might both believe in a general European war and there might be a war, but I at forty-five and my son at seventeen, no Mademoiselle. It is not logical. But, I said, that is alright for you, the French are a logical people, but the Germans and the Italians. Mademoiselle, he said, they talk differently but they believe the same.

Well he went away and then in almost ten days he came back and there he was on the road with his wife and his oxen, and I walking with my dogs met him. I said, Monsieur Lambert you were right there was no war. No he said no Mademoiselle it is not logical.

To-day and now there is a war I met them and I said I was noticing how tall the boy was, he is bigger than his father. Alas yes said the mother, he is eighteen and will the war last and take him. She was not crying, she was thinking. Monsieur Lambert is right therefore logic is logic and perhaps after all it will not be a general European war, and not a real war.

So there are the two sides to a Frenchman, logic and fashion and that is the reaon why French people are exciting and peaceful.

Logic and fashion.

Then they also say it is war and we must help each other, in France they must not help each other in peace-time, the joy of peace is that everybody can take care of themselves that is of their unit as a family.

That is another interesting thing about French people, that they know that.

It is difficult to go back to 1901 now that it is 1939 and war-time.

But at that time 1901 one day at dinner everybody was talking about war, it was war-time then only it was a Russian Japanese war. The servant who was waiting at table suddenly heard some one say that the enemy had just won a battle,—she was carrying a large platter and she dropped it and cried out oh is it the Germans who have come. Naturally war only meant to her Germans.

Of course it is awful to be always under the threat of war and yet does it do something about logic and fashion that is interesting.

Is it possible that America does not know that the world is round because there is no threat of war. To be sure they have had a good many wars but they have had no threat of war. Wars and threat of wars are different things and threat of war does perhaps help to logic and fashion.

Do Americans perhaps think the world is flat because of their continent just as Europe knows it is round because Columbus sailed from Europe to prove it and even if he did hit up against a flat continent he was sure of it. Russia and America do have a tendency to think the world is not round but it is, but logic and fashion know that it is round and they also know that it does go around and around.

So once more back to the beginning of the twentieth century of France and Paris and everybody in it and of it.

But still now it is 1939 and war-time, well it was just beginning and everything was agitating and one day we were with our friends the Daniel-Rops they are our neighbors in the country and he was expecting a call to go to Paris and the telephone rang. He went quickly to answer it, he was away some time and we were all anxious. He came back. We said what is it. He said the quenelles the Mère Mollard was making for us have gone soft.

Quenelles, well quenelles are the special dish of this country made of flour and eggs and shredded fish or chicken and pounded by the hour and then rolled and then hardened in the cold air and then cooked in a sauce and they are good.

We all laughed we regretted the quenelles but it was French of her with a son at the front to be worried about her quenelles.

Cooking like everything else in France is logic and fashion.

The French are right when they claim that French cooking is an art and is part of their culture because it is based on latin Roman cooking and has been influenced by Italy and Spain. The crusades only brought them new material, it did not introduce into France the manner of cooking and very little was changed.

French cooking is traditional, they give up the past with difficulty in fact they never do give it up and when they have had reforms so called in the seventeenth century and in the nineteenth century, they only accepted it when it became really a fashion in Paris, but when they took something from the outside like the Polish baba brought by Stanislas Leczinski, the father-in-law of Louis XV or the Austrian croissant brought by Marie Antoinette, they took it over completely so completely that it became French so completely French that no other nation questions it. By the way the Austrian croissant was hurriedly made at the siege of Vienna in 1683 by the Polish soldiers of Sobieski to replace the bread that was missing and they called it the crescent the emblem of the Turks whom they were fighting.

Catherine de Medici in the sixteenth century brought cooks with her and made desserts fashionable, complicated Italian desserts, before that there had been nothing sweet in France except fruits. It was in 1541 that at a ball she introduced these desserts into Paris.

During the time of Henry the Fourth they went back to simple foods as he called himself the king of Gonesse where the best bread in France was made.

The French did though have ideas that one is apt to think of as American and Oriental, roasted ducks with oranges, and stuffed turkeys with raspberries, they ate the turkeys young, and a salad with nuts and apples in the time of Louis XIV.

Cook books were best sellers in France through the seventeenth century and in the introduction to the Dons de Comus, 1739, it was said that " the modern kitchen is a kind of chemistry," so it is evident that cooking in France always was logic and fashion and tradition, which is French.

The ice-creams that came from Italy were water-ices that were soft but they the French with that basis made a solid ice-cream which afterwards they themselves called Neapolitan, which is their way.

The logic of the French cooking is that they used all their material in as complicated ways as they knew and this was refined by foreign influences which became the fashion until the death of Louis the fourteenth and under the Regency they had a full burst of inspired French completely French cooks and cooking, the regent himself had a set of silver casseroles and he did his cooking with his courtiers and it was said that the silver casseroles were not more valuable than the things he put in them. More than half of the dishes of the present great cooking of France were created by the court, the men and the women, the great mistresses of that period were either very religious or very great cooks and sometimes both, the great men around the court were all interested in cooking.

The dishes created by them were named after them, to be sure frequently it was their cooks who really created them but it was the courtier who got the credit and made them the fashion.

Louis XV made his own coffee, he never allowed any one else to make his coffee.

The thing that was particular about all the dishes of that period was the sauces, these dishes practically all were famous because of their sauces, the cooking of the dish was important but the sauce was its creation. The material for the forcemeat of these dishes was developed enormously at this period.

Another thing they discovered then was the use of yolks of eggs for thickening their sauces instead of bread crumbs, and this as is easily seen revolutionised cooking and sauces. This was a purely French invention.

The Revolution of course stopped cooking and under Napoleon who did not know what he was eating, he rarely expressed a preference but he asked his cook to give him some flat sausages, his cook disgusted prepared an elaborate dish of finely chopped ingredients, Napoleon ate it without knowing they were not sausages.

But at that moment to save French cooking, Antonin Careme began cooking and he is the creator of present French cooking, but of course much simplified now because then neither material nor work was of any importance.

He made a juice an essence to use in sauces of beef veal and five turkeys and that only should produce a quart of juice.

Traditional again, he went back to the elaborate set dishes really almost of mediaeval France and the Renaissance, but their flavor was elaborated and refined by all the material for cooking that had come into the country since.

Under Louis-Napoleon the writers and poets became the appreciators and critics of cooking as well as the financiers and the court, so Dumas wrote a cook-book, and this went on until the siege of Paris by the Germans and there in the cellars they cooked as elaborately as they knew how to disguise the queer things they had to eat.

When the restaurants became fashionable in the middle of the seventeenth century anybody who had money enough went and in that way learned how to eat, the restaurants had great cooks and really it was through the restaurants that good cooking and fashion in cooking was always diffused throughout France.

The restaurants continued the tradition of popularising complicated and fine cooking that could hardly be done in a simple kitchen and all this until the beginning of the republic after the siege of Paris when everybody more or less at some time even the smallest of the middle classes would be conscious of the great dishes of the French cooking even if not greatly cooked. But in many places they still did cook greatly as well as make the great dishes and that brings me to the Paris I first knew when the Café Anglais still existed.

At the Café Anglais their pride in French cooking expressed itself in the perfection of simple dishes, a saddle of mutton so perfectly and so delicately roasted that in itself it became peaceful and exciting, a roast chicken at Voisin's of the same perfection, sauces instead of being elaborate in these places became simple and perfect, this was in the beginning of the twentieth century.

At the same time as there existed these restaurants who had turned perfect elaboration into perfect simplicity there were the restaurants for the middle classes whose simplicity was beginning to be rather heavy, and the cooking for the lower classes, where simplicity was beginning to be a little too plain and everybody naturally did still talk about cooking.

The hush that always falls when in a French dining-room or in a French restaurant a new dish is presented no matter how poor how rich how simple or how complicated the dish is did still always come but Paris did a little disappoint the provincials when they came to Paris.

I remember being told by a French woman that she could remember when she was a child and they lived in the provinces, the wonder and the awe when Parisians came and brought with them some food from Paris. Now she said the Parisians buy everything they can in the shape of cake or a dish to take with them to Paris. The provinces were having a higher standard of cooking than the capital.

So cooking was decidedly falling off in that period just before the war, they still talked about it, the hush before the new dish was still there, the provinces still had good food, but Paris food was not delicate and perfect any more. And then there was the war.

After the war there was the Americanisation of France, automobiles which kept them from staying at home, cocktails, the worry of spending money instead of saving it, because spending money is always a worry to French people, if they can save life is interesting, if they spend life is dull, and then the introduction of electric stoves and the necessity of not cooking too long, in short French cooking went out and there were very few houses practically none in Paris where cooking was considered an art.

And then slowly it began again. People would begin to talk about some little town far away where a woman cooked, really cooked and everybody would go there no matter how far away it was, the Club of the Hundred formed itself to encourage cooking, the Club of the Four Hundred went beyond the Club of the Hundred.

There was Madame Bourgeois in a little lost town

in the centre of France. She and her husband who had been servants in one of the homes in France that still cared for cooking had inherited a little café in this little town that was not on the road to anywhere not even on a railroad. And she began to cook, nobody came except a few fishermen and the local tradesmen and every day she cooked her best dinner for them and then one day after two years of this, a man from Lyon came by accident, a lawyer, and he was pleased with his dinner and he asked her if she could undertake to cook for a dozen of them who were going to celebrate the legion of honor of one of them and she said yes, and from then on the place was famous and she always tired as she was cooked with the same perfection.

The cooking was simple the twentieth century seemed to want it simple but it was less delicate and a bit richer than the last of the great Paris restaurants.

And so it was the time for the provinces to give the fashion to Paris.

There was no longer a Paris cuisine, there was regional cooking and Paris had to learn from the provinces instead of the provinces learning from Paris.

Last September 1938 when the war did not come one of our friends in the country here, a great cook and a great gourmet, was mobilised a captain of reserve and he had a whole garrison to organise. And I have a charming photograph of him, snapped by a stray visitor, a Polish journalist, he is looking violently at a soldier and the conversation was this. Will you, said Captain d'Aiguy, make us a good risotto, I cannot, my captain, said the soldier who was a cook in one of the big restaurants in Paris, because I have not the foundation of a sauce. Foundation for a sauce, said the captain pale with fury, you have material to cook with, everything you want and you cannot make your sauce you have to have a foundation, what do you mean by a foundation. If you please, said the trembling cook, in Paris we always have a foundation for a sauce and we put that in and then mix the sauce. Yes said Captain d'Aiguy and it tastes like it. Let me teach you French cooking. You have the material and you make your sauce.

Well now the war has commenced again 1939 and the soldiers are all talking about their food, and perhaps when they come back there will be a new outburst of French cooking, it was preparing, the foreign influences after the 1914 war have worn themselves off and now everybody is staying at home again and so naturally they will think about cooking.

When you first really get to know the French one

of the first things that puzzles you is the insistence upon their latinity. They do not consider Italians or Spaniards latin, but they the french are latin, they insist upon being Gauls but all the same they are latin. Finally I realised that what they meant was that the spirit of latinity was kept purer by them the Gallo-Romans than it was in Italy which lost its latinity when they were overcome by barbarians and never recreated it, they might take on the forms and symbols of Rome but essentially the latin culture went out of Italy and it never existed in Spain so its true home has been France. And there is a good deal of truth in it all. At first I did not know what they were talking about but gradually I did begin to feel what they meant by their latinity.

They meant of course logic, the only people who were interested in logic were the Romans, logic because logical people are never brutal, they are never sentimental, they are never careless, they are never intimate, in short they are peaceful and exciting, that is to say they are French. The French understand war because they are logical, they do not care to go to war because they are logical, and to be logical is to be latin. That is what I was gradually understanding. It took me a long time to really understand it.

To be latin was to be civilized to be logical and to be fashionable and the French were and they knew it. They explained it in so many ways that it took a long time to realise it, and perhaps it was in their description of their education that I understood it best.

The relation of the French to Napoleon is perhaps the most curious thing in them, because Napoleon was only latin insofar as he was a soldier, he was not civilized he was not logical and he was not fashionable. It is really the only time in their history that they have not been completely French, but that was natural enough, the revolution had sentimentalised them and strangely enough it was not until the romantic movement came that they once more became French. Napoleon because he was not French had a glamour for them and beside they then had for the only time in their history an idea of propaganda of trying to make other people think as they were thinking. Propaganda is not French, it is not civilized to want other people to believe what you believe because the essence of being civilised is to possess yourself as you are, and if you possess yourself as you are you of course cannot possess any one else, it is not your business. It is because of this element of civilization that Paris has always been the home of all foreign artists, they are friendly, the

PRIERE DE VOLTAIRE.

⁎

O Dieu qu'on méconnait, O Dieu que tout annonce,

Entends lês derniers mots que ma bouche prononce.

Si je me suis trompé, c'est en cherchant ta loi :

Mon cœur peut s'égarer, mais il est plein de toi.

Je vois sans m'alarmer l'Eternité paraitre ;

Et je ne puis penser qu'un Dieu qui m'a fait naitre,

Qu'un Dieu qui sur mes jours versa tant de bienfaits,

Quand mes jours sont éteints, me tourmente à jamais.

French, they surround you with a civilised atmosphere and they leave you inside of you completely to yourself. And their logic too makes it impossible to be propagandists. If there is one thing in the world that is not logical it is propaganda, and also it is the one thing in the world that has nothing to do with fashion. The difference between propaganda and fashion is very interesting.

I like to listen to French people tell about their education. Everybody in France naturally tells about their education, because after all education inevitably has to do with civilisation. They tell you, I remember René Crevel telling about his education, what effect the lycée has upon them, it does not make them a type in character or in manner as similar schools do with the Northern peoples but it has to do simply with the mind. Francois d'Aiguy says lycées because they were founded by Napoleon stamp your mind, the collège or the boîte the catholic schools because they form your character do not form your mind. So which will you have. The discussion of this matter is unending and it always comes back to the question of latinity. At the same time you have the pride in being of peasant stock and the pride in being always in their youth ripe for revolution. I remember Lolo whom we loved very much who always said I am a peasant, well I suppose he might have been but was he. He was a peasant, so he said, he was young and so he was a revolutionary, so he said, and whatever he admired he called with a fine rolling voice, royale. He explained a great deal about revolutions.

He said all French men had to be revolutionary, that is they had to be in revolt, no matter what it was they had they had to be in revolt, not for publicity but for civilization. How could you be civilised if you had not passed through a period of revolt, and then you had to return to your pre-revolt stage and there you were you were civilised. All Frenchmen know that you have to become civilised between eighteen and twenty-three and that civilization comes upon you by contact with an older woman, by revolution, by army discipline, by any escape or by any subjection, and then you are civilised and life goes on normally in a latin way, life is then peaceful and exciting, life is then civilised, logical and fashionable in short life is life.

That is one of the troubles Frenchmen of the post-war generation had in what was called the epoch. It was a Frenchman who said it to me, he said war is not civilising and the men who were eighteen to twenty-three in the war missed their time for becoming civilised. War can not civilise, it takes private life to civilize, and of course publicity has the same effect as war it prevents the process of civilization.

That was really the trouble with the sur-realist crowd, they missed their moment of becoming civilised, they used their revolt, not as a private but as a public thing, they wanted publicity not civilisation, and so really they never succeeded in being peaceful and exciting, they did not succeed in the real sense in being fashionable and certainly not in being logical. This does bring me back to Paris from 1900 to 1939.

Some one was telling me the other day who knew Debussy very well, that Debussy prided himself on being a peasant of course he was not but that is the way he felt about it and on being a French musician. He said that German music stopped with the empire and so French music which was the music of civilization, logic and fashion could naturally begin. He was not supposed to have said quite that but that is what he meant.

He also said that the empire was manifestly not healthy for Germany because music was not doing anything, it tailed off with Strauss. He was also said to have said that Eric Satie had an extraordinary endowment but he could not work. He being a peasant believed in work. Any peasant does.

French life has elements of strangeness in it. In France a young girl is treated as a young girl, she is a young girl until she is a married woman when she is not any longer a young girl, but and, this is extraordinary, a young girl of twenty-one or twenty-two becomes a school-teacher, and in France in the country a school-teacher has to live alone in the school-house. A young girl will go into a mountain village or a village in the plains, or a village anywhere and the school-house is never in the village but well outside of it quite isolated with its living quarters for the school-teacher, and there she lives alone, she may be very young but there she is living alone in an empty school-house, doing her own work, and feeding herself and living alone.

When I really realised this I was surprised and I said does not that contradict the feeling about a young girl and her protection, no they said, it is understood, and if it is understood to be so nothing happens that should not happen and very evidently nothing does. Even loneliness does not really seem to happen even though the school-house may be in a village in the mountains snowed in for long months.

It surprised us but it did not surprise the French.

And back again to the twentieth century.

The characteristic thing of the twentieth century was the idea of production in a series, that one thing should be like every other thing, and that it should all be made alike and quantities of them. As I said the impressionists had the idea that a painting should be painted every day indeed preferably two a day, morning and afternoon. That was the nineteenth century, and then the twentieth century believed that painting should be completely subjective and not objective, that thoughts should be painted and not things seen. And so naturally even more than even one painting a day or two or even four could be painted because complete thoughts come all the time and each time any of them thought they thought a thought and this thought being painted was complete.

The twentieth century was not interested in impressions, it was not interested in emotions it was interested in conceptions and so there was the twentieth century painting.

These conceptions all have to do with the world being round and everybody knowing all about it and there being illimitable space and everybody knowing all about it and if anybody knows all about the world being round and all about illimitable space the first thing they do is to paint their conceptions of these things and that the twentieth century painting did.

But, and this is very important the French background never did disassociate itself from the earth, the world is all round and everybody knows all about it, but even if they do, there it still is the ground, it is still there.

They the french were the only ones who really knew it was still there, even though it was in France that twentieth century art and literature is made.

I was very pleased one day when the wife of the local doctor, he and she are fond of digging a bit and here when you dig a bit, beside making things grow, there is Roman, and Gallo-Roman, and even earlier things to be found. Well one day we were out in the car and she said one day when the workmen were first cutting this road through there on that ledge were the ancestors, lots of their bones. It is always there life and death death and life and the earth and it is never anything to be remembered or even talked about, and that is the reason the French do not make much lyrical poetry. They do not get away from the earth enough to look at it, they paint it, but they do not poetise it.

As always art is the pulse of a nation. I was just thinking of a good title for an art book. From Bismark to Hitler, any one can see that since 1870 and to 1939 Germany has had no art. When a country is in such a state that people who like to buy things can find nothing to buy there is something wrong.

Once when I was crossing the American continent, years and years ago and we were caught in the prairies without an engine to take us anywhere, the news-agent who sold things on the train came and offered us ten bananas for ten cents and then added, when a news-agent offers you ten bananas for ten cents you know there is something wrong.

That is the state of a nation when there is no art that is natural to that nation, you know there is something wrong. Ever since Germany has been an empire there has been nothing anybody wanted to buy and after having bought wanted to leave to a museum, neither music nor pottery nor poetry, and so there is something wrong. The state of being an empire was not a healthy state.

There is a very interesting thing in this connection.

France naturally was never interested in English painting and only very recently there was a collection shown of Blake and Turner. The French were astonished, they felt that somehow here was something that the later twentieth century needed. The painting of the young Englishman Francis Rose affected a good many of us the same way, after all if you know that the world is round and that space is unlimited well why talk about it any more. Facts are facts. It is a fact and so let us know it but not remember it. All great facts should be known but not remembered like the earth to the French, and so for the first time for a long time the phenomena of nature, thunder and storms and mountains and birds were things to live among. The English who naturally do live in among these things but in the confusion of refusing the twentieth century had lost their vitality of creating them they the English were once more finding the new thing in their old thing, in the thing that was natural to them and so in this war 1939 they are coming into their own, ideas are not important but light and loveliness is important.

The French with their feeling for fashion know that the English have found themselves again and they say Cette fois nous avons un allié, les Anglais.

Gravé par Mme Lamothe

Janvier 1801

PENSÉE DE J.J. ROUSSEAU.

L'Etre Eternel ne se voit, ni ne s'entend; il se fait sentir; il ne parle ni aux yeux, ni aux oreilles, mais au cœur. nous pouvons bien disputer contre son essence infinie, mais non pas le méconnoitre de bonne foi. Moins je le conçois, plus je l'adore. je m'humilie et lui dis : Etre des Etres, je suis parceque tu es, c'est m'élever à ma source, que de méditer sans cesse. le plus digne usage de ma raison est de s'anéantir devant toi : c'est mon ravissement d'esprit, c'est le charme de ma foiblesse de me sentir accablé de ta grandeur.

PART IV

I LIKE WORDS of one syllable and it works out very well in the French order for general mobilisation. The printed thing gives all the detail and then it says the army de terre, de mer et de l'air. That is very impressive when you read it in every village.

It could be a puzzle why the intellectuals in every country are always wanting a form of government which would inevitably treat them badly, purge them so to speak before anybody else is purged. It has always happened from the French revolution to to-day. It would be a puzzle this if it were not that it is true that the world is round and that space is illimitable unlimited. I suppose it is that that makes the intellectual so anxious for a regimenting government which they could so ill endure.

And so war comes and it has its advantages, it does make a concentration of isolation, there are so many more people, animals and fowls and children in war-time than in peace-time, but it does all make for a concentration of isolation and this is interesting.

And old French friend, Madame Pierlot once said

to me she is now eighty-eight and she said that she is so much more flattered now than when she was a fascinating young woman. Fitzgerald once said to me it is easy to charm the old. But that is not the whole story it is easy for the old to charm.

Perhaps this war will make ages reasonable again, the last war completely destroyed ages, and I suppose life inevitably is calmer if there are ages.

Which makes this war real again. Uniforms say the French make every one younger and then when you take the uniform off it makes everybody just that much older. In the last war uniforms were worn so long that that consciousness was lost but now more uniforms come off and on, mobilisation and demobilisation takes place more frequently, as Bernard Fay just wrote I have come back to Paris and so many of my friends have been demobilised and it makes them feel rather sheepish.

And so ages have come into existence again.

But then there was the mistake about Kiki Vincent.

Madame Chaboux told it to me. It is she who cooked jugged hare better than anybody else in the region, and it was she who told how she and her husband and two friends went to an inn for dinner where they made a specialty of jugged hare and as the dish was presented to them and the hush fell upon them the hush with which French people always receive a dish, the friend half crying said but they have not left us any morceaux ronds, there was nothing there but shoulders and legs and heads, there were no round pieces, the round pieces that so deliciously are made by the centre of the animal. So now we never see a jugged hare without thinking of the morceaux ronds whose non-appearance is a poignant grief.

We met Madame Chaboux coming out of the garrison barracks, what said we are you doing there, ah she said I went to see the captain about Kiki, Kiki Vincent.

So when we wanted to know she told us.

The woman at the market who sells butter and cheese always used, before the 1939 war, always used to come in a wagon drawn by a white horse. And now there was war, horses had been requisitioned and she came in an old automobile. Madame Chaboux bought her butter and cheese and asked if all the family were well, and the butter-woman began to drop tears on the cheese. All she said except Kiki. But they have not taken Kiki said Madame Chaboux, oh but they have was the answer, he was twenty years old the good horse Kiki but he did not look his age, he always appeared youthful and so when they were taking horses, we had no proof he was twenty but he was twenty and he used to put his head out of the stable just opposite to my kitchen and we used to talk together and my husband says it is nothing but he is suffering and the children when we go out they say where is Kiki Vincent, will he come back and of course although he looked so young he was twenty and of course he will not come back. Madame Chaboux said that if she had his number she would see if he could be found perhaps he had not gone far, so she went to see the captain with the number, 73726 and underneath written Kiki on a piece of paper, and there were two horses there that had not gone yet but they had a different number and she had their numbers too on a piece of paper, 72943 and 74056 but they were not Kiki. The captain said if he had only known in time he could have saved Kiki but now Kiki was gone.

I have the two pieces of paper with the numbers but Kiki is gone, and army life is hard on horses so Kiki Vincent is gone.

The French like to call beasts up-to-date names, names of people do not change much but they like to follow the fashion in animal's names.

It always pleases me that French boys are often called Jean-Marie, you can use a female name to go with a man's name, it hallows the male name to add the female name to it, and that is civilised and logical and might be fashionable, it has always existed.

But the animals' names are a different matter, there are all the regular names and then there are other ones. I remember the pleasure in hearing a farmer call one of his oxen Landru, is it really his name I asked oh yes, he said, but not because he is a murderer, oh no, he said, just to like it. Of course most female dogs are called Diane, that is inevitable, but all the terriers have English names, they are called Jimmie and Tom and one is known as Nickey Boy de Belley.

Our dog's name is Basket and the French like that, it sounds well in French and goes very well with Monsieur, the children all call him Monsieur Basket more or less to rhyme with casquette.

That was the first Basket.

We did love the first Basket and he was shaved like a real poodle and he did fait le beau and he could say how do you do and he was ten years old and last autumn just after our return to Paris he died. We did cry and cry and finally every one said get another dog and get it right away.

Henry Daniel-Rops said get another as like Basket as possible call him by the same name and gradually there will be confusion and you will not know which Basket it is. They had done that twice with their little white Teneriffe which they call Claudine.

And then I saw Picasso, and he said no, never get the same kind of a dog again never, he said I tried it once and it was awful, the new one reminded me of the old one and the more he looked like him the worse it was. Why said he, supposing I were to die, you would go out on the street and sooner or later you would meet a Pablo, but it would not be I and it would be the same. No never get the same kind of a dog, get an Afghan hound, he has one, and Jean Hugo had said I could have one, but they are so sad, I said, that's all right for a Spaniard, but I don't like dogs to be sad, well he said get what you like but not the same, and as I went out he repeated not the same no not the same.

So we tried to have the same and not to have the same and there was a very large white poodle offered to us who looked like a young calf with black spots and other very unpleasant puppies with little pink eyes and then at last we found another Basket, and we got him and we called him Basket and he is very gay and I cannot say that the confusion between the old and the new has yet taken place but certainly le roi est mort vive le roi, is a normal attitude of mind.

I was a little worried what Picasso would say when he saw the new Basket who was so like the old Basket but fortunately the new Basket does stand on his legs in some indefinable way a little the way an Afghan hound stands on his although Basket the new Basket is pure poodle, and I pointed this out to Picasso when we and our dogs met on the street and that did rather reconcile him to it.

It is rather interesting that the Frenchman said have the same and the Spaniard said no don't have the same. The Frenchman does realise the inevitability of le roi est mort vive le roi but the Spaniard does not recognise the inevitability of resemblances and continuation. He just does not but a Frenchman just does.

And now this Basket being a war-dog, that is living in the country with us all the time in war-time is very much a village dog and although the village spends a great deal of time discussing whether he is more or less beautiful than the last one, whether he is bigger and whether he is more affectionate the children like him but they treat him with less respect, they call him Basket familiarly they do not call him Monsieur Basket, there is that difference in their character, I mean the character of this Basket and that Basket. But for all that he is a very sweet Basket, any dog one loves is a very sweet dog and poor Madame Pierlot has just lost her Jimmie, and he was just the same age as the other Basket.

Names are always interesting, and in this morning's local paper I found that Mademoiselle Pierette Davignon, ex-modiste has just died at eighty-one years of age.

It is a very wonderful name that, Mademoiselle Pierette Davignon.

It really takes a war to make you know a country, I had only known Paris until 1914 and then I learned to know France, and now once again living here all winter in a provincial French town I once more realise that a war brings you in contact with so much and so many and at the same time concentrates your isolation. Undoubtedly that is what a war does and is it unconsciously one of the things that makes wars happen, this thing.

After all human beings are like that. When they are alone they want to be with others and when they are with others they want to be alone and war in a kind of way concentrating all this destroys it and intensifies it.

Well war does make one realise the march of centuries and the succession of generations.

The nineteenth century wars were invented by the citizens of the first French republic. They invented a nation in arms, Napoleon rather spoiled it all, he went back to pre-revolutionary fighting, did it very well but after all it was eighteenth century and not nineteenth century fighting, Wellington as a matter of fact was more nineteenth century than Napoleon, his Spanish campaign was much more nineteenth century warfare than anything Napoleon did. And so the French having invented nineteenth century warfare and then lost it, it was completed by the Americans in their civil war, they developed and fixed it as a thing definite and complete and the 1914–1918 war was as one might say just the end of the series. It was just at the end of that war that Trotzky defined the twentieth century war, which is neither war nor peace, it was he that said it, he invented it as the French republicans invented the nineteenth century war but in inventing it they lost it. The Nazis and the Soviets like Napoleon lost the thing that was found and now England and France as the Americans in the civil war, in 1939 have recreated and realised the twentieth century war.

It is very interesting. They have found the secret of not war and not peace but with it they will have found the way to victory and to peace. And a new Europe. Anyway that is the way I feel about it.

It is very interesting about England and France, they have been completely conscious of each other for such a very long time, sometimes in one way sometimes in another way but always completely conscious of each other.

Now it is war-time and the families who usually spend their winter in cities are all spending them in the country. We too.

Naturally they all study at home, particularly the young girls, because at this time the French family prefer that the young girls are under their own roof and so everybody studies as best they can. They naturally all want to learn English just now and quite naturally we all talk about that. Some of these girls have already passed their first baccalaureate and some are now preparing for their second and in this second they must translate a whole English thing into French. They are given a choice of Hamlet, Paradise Lost, some of the essayists and Emerson, and they all without any hesitation chose Hamlet. They like it best and they think it is the easiest to do.

I was looking over Hamlet with one of them and I was very much struck particularly in the ghost scene, that all the words which are no longer in use are French words completely French words, and I could see why they all felt that it was easy to translate because there they were all these completely French words which were there for them and which the English language to-day no longer uses.

I have often thought a lot about the words that make the English language, and much as I have thought about it, a war makes it even more definite, as in this Hamlet.

Of course it was pure French and pure Saxon and then less pure French and more Latin than French until in the nineteenth century one quite has ceased to feel the French in the English.

All this time of course the French and English have always been keenly conscious of each other until the nineteenth century, after the Napoleonic wars they for quite a long time were not conscious of each other, each one conducted the nineteenth century in their own way until toward the end of the nineteenth century, when France did not find the century particularly interesting and England was beginning to refuse the twentieth century which was on the way, France and England once more became livelily conscious of each other which culminated in 1914–1918.

Up to that time France was still interested in either the nineteenth or the twentieth century and England was still clinging to the nineteenth and refusing the twentieth.

One might say that America which represented the twentieth century and Russia which hoped for the twentieth century did not interest either France or England very much and the twentieth century as conceived by these two countries did not please them, did not please either the civilisation the logic or the fashion of the French and did not please the civilisation, the idealism, or the rationality of the English and so neither France nor England were really interested in the twentieth century. The 1914–1918 war changed all this. These two countries realised that the twentieth century should not get out of their hands, that they had to make of it for the French a thing logical civilised and fashionable and the English had to manage it in their fashion, for after all civilisation was in their hands and without them the world would not be civilised and so they had to come into the twentieth century and make it civilised and here we are now.

You can see that the long line of English writers every twenty-nine years a man of genius suffered during this period when England refused the twentieth century and that is most interesting because one must never forget that the characteristic art product of a country is its pulse and in England it is prose and poetry.

I never get over the pleasure of the use of French as it is used by anybody French. In this village we have all shades of opinion and there is the Rosset family very Catholic very conservative, not royalist because they are republican but great believers in tradition.

I remember one day it was the fourteenth of July and just the year of the Front Commun, and I happened to meet Monsieur Rosset and I said are you going in town, and he said why should I go in town. Well said I meekly it is the fourteenth of July.

The fourteenth of July he said, the fall of the Bastille, quelle masquerade. I can give no impression of the word masquerade as it came out of him. I realised what a feeble word the English word spelled just the same really was.

And now Georges is aux armées, and the father who adores Georges is very severe about how inevitably you have to kill a million men to win a war.

Georges writes to me, I hear just at this moment that we are leaving to-morrow for the front that is for a destination unknown. Let us guard our courage and hope that very soon we will be again in Bilignin and with our friends.

These are the typical French farmers.

And in the village of Bilignin we have had several alerts. And there are two schools of thought.

Madame Votarey says that we are among mountains, actually they are very high hills, we are in the foothills of the French Alps and she says that it is easy to lose your way in among mountains particularly if you are in the air, so how could they find Bilignin. Beside anyway she had made up her mind not to be evacuated, and Madame Chanel says that since airplanes must necessarily go here and there they may easily sometime come here. At any rate adds she reflectively men are fond of fighting. They are unreasonable, if it rains too much they want to fight, anything will make men fight. Anyway she adds we are free in France.

Madame Pierlot is very much interested in the way the men come back on leave looking so very large and so very fat. She says in her eighty-eight years it is the first war she has ever known that men on leave come back looking so very large and so very healthy and so very fat. The women whether it is by contrast or because they have to work so hard look very thin beside them.

The twentieth century wars might easily make men healthy and fat because certainly the twentieth century has made a great difference in the French country, ours is a mountain village but there are no poor, they are all comfortable and they all have some luxuries, they all have bicycles they all have good clothes for Sunday, they all have jam to put on their bread, they all have plenty of chickens and ducks which they do not sell but eat themselves and they all have money in the bank, which they call argent liquide. In the country here they say the milk pays their current expenses, their calves pay taxes and extra things like births marriages and deaths and the wheat they eat, and the wine makes the money they put in the bank and the potatoes they eat. In this way they say anybody can be comfortable and you have plenty of wine and meat and butter and bread to eat. In this whole countryside there is only one family not completely comfortable and they are not poor but they are neglected, there are four small children in the family all the same size but different ages which happens when children are neglected. The war brought them new clothes, the chanoine at Belley wanted to do something and he gave them a complete outfit, to go to school, they always go to school of course but this time they went completely new, even as they told me, to their underclothes, they seem to think new clothes naturally come when there is a war.

Even in Belley which is comparatively a city, it having a population of about five thousand and it is an important place, even there there are no poor. They have a bazaar de charité once every two years and the money they gather goes to general things, rather than specific aid, there is a very large home for the aged of the region but there are not many in it. I was talking about this the other day to the Duke of Clermont-Tonnerre, he was staying with Madame Pierlot across the valley, and he said yes it is true. He said in the part of the country he lives in, which is quite a different kind of country, it was also true. He could well remember when he was a boy that it was not so then there were many very poor in the country. I asked him if he thought the 1914 war had something to do with the change, a little he said, it did certainly accelerate it, but actually it had commenced before 1914. So it was the twentieth century all alone that did it.

We have had here in the village a little girl and her name is Hélène Bouton, Helen Button, and I have been kind of wondering just what a child's feeling about war-time is. It is very interesting.

This is the way I have been feeling this, because after all this war is not war, it is war-time.

Helen Button was her name and she lived in war-

LA BARONNE PIERLOT   *Landscape near Belley*

time. She lived somewhere but the thing that is important is that she lived during war-time.

There is a great deal of war-time in history and Helen Button lived in it.

In this war-time the sun did shine it does do that but Helen Button always knew that it was going to rain before evening and it did do that, she knew it by signs, she did not know what the signs were but she knew by signs that it was going to rain.

In war-time children dogs and chickens are either frightened or they are naughtier than usual, either one or the other. And there are rather more of them more of chickens dogs and children than before. Helen Button knew this. And a dog was more likely to kill a chicken in war-time than in peace-time. Helen Button's dog did not kill one but he did find a dead one and he brought it to her and laid it down in front of her. Helen was worried that they might think that he had killed a chicken, so she and the cook secretly cooked and ate the chicken so no one would suspect the dog. This could only have happened to Helen in war-time.

Of course children do go in and out as they like a great deal more in war-time than in peace-time for there is not much use in just staying at home while it is war-time.

Helen Button started out with her dog William. As they were walking along suddenly William stopped and was very nervous. He saw something on the road and so did Helen. They neither of them knew what it was at first and at last as they approached very carefully they saw it was a bottle, a bottle standing up right in the middle of the road. There had been something in the bottle but what, it looked dark green or may be blue or black, and the bottle was standing up in the middle of the road not lying on its side the way a bottle on the road usually is.

William the dog and Helen the little girl went on. They did not look back at the bottle. But of course it was still there because they had not touched it.

That is war-time.

When Helen went out there were a great many little boys on large bicycles about. The bicycles were so tall that they could not get on the seats at all but they were all over the country wriggling from side to side to have their ride and when they saw any water and some of the roads were under water they went forward and back through the water to make it splash. That was because their big brothers and their fathers were gone away and that made so many more little boys able to play.

Then Helen did know it was war-time.

Helen and her dog William were out every day and almost every evening and they always saw some one. They knew a boy named Emil who was a big boy with very large eyes and a dog named Ellen. Ellen the dog had been born in the country against which they were fighting. Emil looked at his dog and wondered if he could love him. The dog loved Emil but could Emil love him.

As Helen and her dog William came along Emil's dog Ellen was sniffing along the side of the road in the sand and finally went sniffing up the bank. Helen's dog William went sniffing too. Perhaps there was game there, very likely because in war-time men did not go shooting nobody hunted anything only dogs and cats hunted in war-time, Emil the boy with large eyes sighed about this. He said dogs hunt in war-time but they do not get much, anybody could see two or three dogs going together to hunt and waiting to see if anybody saw them because in peace-time of course they could not go hunting. Then Emil said but cats in peace-time or in war-time, they sit and watch and prey.

It was getting darker and beginning to rain and Helen went one way and Emil went another way and each one of their dogs went with the one who owned him.

Helen had a grandmother and when she had been the age of Helen there had been war-time. She told Helen how one day she had a slice of bread and there was very little bread to be had, but she did have a good big slice and she was just commencing eating it. A soldier came along an enemy soldier on a horse, he stopped and got off his horse and not roughly but he did, he took the slice of bread out of her hand, she had just had one bite and he gave it to his horse who ate it and he went away on his horse and he did not say anything.

It was war-time now but Helen had bread whenever she wanted it and butter on it and she had jam and honey and yet it was war-time.

School did not commence as soon as usual, it always did commence as the days were shorter and now the days were shorter and everything was darker and darker and there were no lights and Helen and her dog began to walk in the dark and she could see the road in the dark and she knew it was war-time. She did think about its being war-time but she knew it was.

Helen Button thought that in war-time there was not any difference between day and night. And she was right. The nights were black and the days were dark and there was no morning. Not in war-time.

So said Helen Button to herself, she did not talk to the cook nor to her mother, she did not talk to Emil the boy who had eyes that were so large, she talked to herself. You do in war-time.

You talk to yourself about chestnuts and walnuts and hazelnuts and beechnuts, you talk to yourself about how many you find and whether they have worms in them. You talk to yourself about apples and pears and grapes and which kind you like best. You just go on talking to yourself in war-time. You talk to yourself about caterpillars but you never talk to yourself about spiders or lizards, you talk to yourself about dogs and cats and rabbits but not about bats or mice or moths.

There are falling stars in war-time and Helen Button saw them. Would stars come tumbling and frighten every one. She saw some stars be blue and some red, she said to herself one star is very red and when that red star turns blue there will not be any more war-time.

Helen knew that Emil's dog was born in the enemy country. It had been given to Emil by some one who came from there long before it was war-time.

One day, it was not at night it was in the morning, Emil was not there but his dog Ellen was there and Helen saw him. It was not true of course, it was not true but Helen said to herself, I was watching and the dog Ellen was changing and her fur turned into large baggy trousers and her head turned into a large shaggy head and it was a man, an enemy man, yes it was said Helen to herself and I saw him and he went down the road and I knew that it was a man, who was an enemy and it was and I saw him.

She met Emil shortly after and his dog was with him but it was not any longer morning and Helen did not look at the dog Ellen, she looked at her own dog William as if she knew him and she did and she knew her own dog would come when she called him.

It was not long after that that every dog had to have a muzzle on him. They used to talk about that on the road. The men had had muzzles on dogs in the country before when dogs might be mad and now it was war-time and the dogs had to have them.

Helen Button listened to everybody and everybody said something different about the reason why but Helen did not say anything but she knew that she knew the reason why.

Emil was just fascinating but so was Helen.

She knew just what was going to happen at least her aunt Pauline did, her aunt was what they called extra-lucid, that meant that she knew what was going to happen, she always had but now in war-time it was much more important. In peace time nothing much did happen so there was no use in knowing what was going to happen but in war-time anything might happen so it was very necessary to know it.

What Helen Button liked best was about the curé d'Ars, she liked all about him, she liked his not having learned his lessons very well when he studied, she liked his being kind to every one and she liked his being a saint and she liked it that her grandmother could remember him. But most she liked that he had said that the day would come when the women would plough the ground and plant the wheat but the men would do the harvesting. And the women she saw them they were sowing the wheat and the men because the curé d'Ars had always known everything they would be back again to do the harvesting, it was war-time but they would be back again. And then she was a little strange when she heard that the nuns in the cities did not wear coiffes any more, they could not and get gas masks over them, so they could not wear them any more and the curé d'Ars had predicted that too. He had said the time would come when the sisters in the hospitals would not wear their coiffes, and of course but still nobody really believed him but now the time had come, they were not wearing them, but and this was consoling every one, he had said that all this would only last for a time a very short time just long enough to turn an omelette. And this was comforting.

Helen Button loved to listen to her aunt Pauline, they called her The Pauline and a good many people did believe her, but really Helen never thought about whether it was so or not. She liked to just say it to Emil when she saw him and she knew saying it made her fascinating.

So Helen knew when the war was going to end and when there would be no more war-time and Helen knew that this did make her fascinating.

Her Aunt Pauline did really know everything. She knew when any enemy was going to be dead, she knew how often a clock would strike, she knew who was not going to eat eggs, she knew who was going to buy a hat, she knew everything.

Helen Button went out with her dog and the moon was shining.

Helen should not have been out when the moon was shining, she knew she should not. She should only have been out when it was dark because if the moon shone it was night not just dark. There she was though and automobiles came quickly in the bright moon-light, they came slowly in the dark because their lights were green and blue not white.

VLAMINCK

La Pompe d'Essence

The automobile came on, it went over William and Helen screamed and William was down and then he was up and then away he went, oh how he did go. Helen went on calling and William came back crawling.

Oh dear where was Emil with eyes so big that he could see everything.

Helen and William did get home and that after all was something.

So war-time just went on being war-time and after that William the dog had a stiff neck but it did not last long he was soon very well but he was always scared when he saw a light and particularly scared when he suddenly saw the moon through the mist and it does look green.

Emil was not an orphan. He had a horse. There were not many of them, most of them had been taken to go to the war. Emil's horse was a heavy one the kind that pulled things, that is perhaps the reason they did not take him, he went ahead too slowly even for war-time.

So it was left to pull things and one day Helen met it, it was pulling a wagon and on the wagon was an animal, nobody had ever seen any animal like it before, it was enormous and it was dead.

The horse pulling the wagon did not mind nor

Emil but Emil's dog Ellen minded very much, very much indeed.

The enormous animal did not have a tail and it did not have any ears. It was an enormous animal and it was war-time.

Helen did not really see it but she told herself about it. She said, dear me.

Nobody knew where the wagon and the horse went, nobody ever does in war-time.

When Helen Button went to sleep she did not dream. Then all of a sudden she began to dream. She dreamed that it was war-time.

When she woke she did not get up, it was war-time and nobody just said to her get up but bye and bye she did get up and she went out. After a while she stood perfectly still and listened.

She thought she heard it but did she.

She listened and listened. It was war-time and so she listened and listened.

She heard weather, she heard water she heard snow, she heard water everywhere, it was that kind of weather. She heard snow around she very nearly heard the moon and she heard the rain and she heard the mountains.

There might be school and Helen might go to school but she did not. Nobody said she should and indeed so few went that any day there might not be a school and so it was anyday and it was war-time. So every day she went out and the snow came and the snow melted and water was everywhere and dogs hunted game not Helen's dog but other dogs and these dogs stood and waited until everybody was out of sight and then they hunted game. Men could not go hunting but dogs could. That is war-time.

One day Helen and her dog and Emil and his dog met going up and up a hill.

They went up and they saw a man there. He was not an old man, he was a young one and it was war-time and seeing a young man in ordinary clothes was startling. This man up there on that hill, there was snow and water there, had a spy glass and he was looking way off through it.

Is he said Helen Yes he is said Emil.

And he was and they said, Helen and Emil, shall we and Emil said yes. Now said Helen. Yes said Emil. And how said Helen. I know him said Emil.

Emil went up to the man. He said to him. You are an enemy. I am not, said the man. If you are not what is your name said Emil. My name is Henry said the man.

There they stood and the snow in the fields and the water splashing and the man in wooden shoes, looking through his spy-glass at something.

What should they do.

It was really war-time.

They all went away always looking behind.

Very soon then there was nobody anywhere.

This is war-time.

Helen did not know why but this was the first thing in war-time that had made her cry.

It was not long after that Emil went away and his dog too. Whether to the war or not Helen never knew.

There are so many people who go away in war-time and there are always so many everywhere in war-time here there and everywhere.

So now it was still war-time and Helen began to go to school too.

So for her war-time was over.

So this is the twentieth century. I have been thinking a lot about centuries. I think centuries are like men, they begin as children begin simple and hopeful then they go through that period that Doctor Osler used to call the senseless age, boys of eleven to seventeen, and then they go through their period of becoming civilised and then the century more or less settles down, becomes as the French say rangé that is civilised and the work is over.

I have a kind of feeling that every century is like that, certainly the nineteenth century was and the twentieth, the other centuries probably were too. What is true in one century is pretty certainly true of all of them.

So here we are in the twentieth century at the moment when the century begins to be ready for civilising.

In the early part of the century, the century like all adolescents and sometimes it lasts considerably longer, long to get away from the family, the real family and the idea of the family.

Every adolescent has that dream every century has that dream every revolutionary has that dream, to destroy the family.

In France, well the dream even among the adolescent intellectuals, the violent revolutionaries, the adolescent communists, it really is not very real. After all every Frenchman knows that he is destined to be a père de famille a father of a family, even if he has neither wife nor child being a père de famille is his manifest destiny. Every Frenchman will inevitably speak of himself and his comrades, nous pères de famille, it is really the only way that a Frenchman can realise life and so although adolescence and intellectualism demand that he believes in a world not based upon a family unit, in his heart every Frenchman knows that that is all there is to it, a family and himself a father of a family.

It is interesting that in the country in almost every village there is a man who has not married, either his mother lived too long and he never got married, or he just did not get married because he was off somewhere and did not get back, anyway for one reason or another not uncommonly in a village there is one man who never got married. Usually even if the mother did live so long and so possessed her son that he grew quite old unmarried, nevertheless when his mother dies some widow marries him but every now and then and very often one in almost any village is unmarried.

Nobody can really take him seriously, they very often call him familiarly, a hen, and most of the time he does go a little funny, he stands sadly around and looks at the women who never became his wife and once in a while he goes quite queer, as recently in a village not far from here, one day he was about fifty-five and he never had been married, he shot a woman just any woman as he saw her at a distance.

No man who had ever been married could have done that, manifestly not.

There are of course some women not often more than one in a village who has not married, but she is not so likely in France to go funny, of course there are always animals, and animals can become a family, to a Frenchwoman, but not to a Frenchman.

In our village there is a woman like that and she loves her dog and the last time it was a blind one, she and her old father and the dog born blind did and do make a family and even when her father dies she will still have a family, because some animal will be treated by her as a member of a family.

Madame Chaboux told me a story about that.

It is perfectly natural in France to say that a little dog was sitting on the lap of his mother. In fact French people are quite convinced French is the only language which has a real baby language for dogs, I remember once a long discussion ending up triumphantly with, in English how could you say, come chien chien come to your mamère.

You do not say to a dog come to your father, a Frenchman but you do say come to your mother, a Frenchwoman.

So Madame Chaboux was in her country in the Jura and she went to a concert given for the soldiers and the country people were all there and next to her was sitting a country woman and on her lap was a little dog. Madame Chaboux in telling the story said quite naturally, next to me a little dog was sitting on the lap of its mother, the little dog was very discreet, when there was applause he woke up and barked a bit but otherwise he was quite quiet. It was announced that the most famous flutist in France happened to be in the country and he had offered to play for the soldiers. He came onto the stage and began to arrange his flute. The mother of the little dog a little uneasy turned to Madame Chaboux and said, pourvu que mon petit chien aime la flute, pourvu. It is to be hoped my little dog will like the flute, it is to be hoped.

That is the French way, no conviction, a hope and that is all.

The French do love to say a thing and say it completely.

That is the reason that once a thing is completely named it does no longer worry them. Now the word une guerre des nerfs, has become a part of their speech, it has no longer any effect upon their nerves. That is their logic fashion and civilisation.

So naturally although the French do have as every country seems to need to have that adolescent intellectualism of the negation of the family in their hearts it is not so. That is one of the reasons that French people are not snobs.

No matter what is the origin of any man, no matter what he has achieved, it never enters his head not to return to the family, the simple countryman can have children in any walk of life and there is no complication, the well dressed man comes to his home where his people are roughly clad and as they were and nobody feels that there is any discrepancy, never at any time.

It is of course also true of the army, anybody can be a simple soldat as anybody can be an officer. It is a question of metier, of a profession, and not of class.

Here in the town, the notary, the lawyer, the banker are all simple soldiers, the son of the butcher is an officer, it is all a question of profession it is not a matter of class.

Pierre Leyris a young writer and neighbor of ours in the country here was speaking of that the other day. He is not very strong and so he is an auxiliare and not in the active army but during mobilisation they were mobilised as a company of auxiliares to be used in helping in the machinery of mobilisation. He enjoyed his short military career, he enjoyed his comrades they all had a good time together, and then mobilisation over, they were demobilised. He said that was a dreadful day. When they put on their civilian clothes it was all different, they looked at each other differently they knew what each one was and when they had been all together, nobody knew or cared.

I remember a French sister in a convent speaking of that too. She said the costume and the coiffe, the coiffe that the curé d'Ars said they would take off for long enough to turn an omelette and which many of them have had to take off to put on the gas masks, well she said we never know what any sister comes from and what her background is unless by accident we are in the parloir seeing our relations and she is in the parloir seeing hers. Then they could know but I imagine they are not supposed to notice.

We saw the Père Abbé of the abbaye royale d'Hautecombe yesterday, sixteen of his twenty-six monks are mobilised, and most of them as simple soldiers. One of them one of the older ones is an aumonier, a priest to an aviation division. He is immensely pleased with himself, he not alone has an automobile and a chauffeur at his disposition but he also has an airplane and an aviator. There was a charming twinkle in the Père Abbé's eye when he told us that.

Madame Giroud herself the widow of a general told us about her family, every ten years they reunite all the family that is in existence and at the last the two most striking members were one of the great judges of France and the driver of a country hearse. But they were all family and they had a good dinner a most excellent dinner all of them together.

Madame Giroud told us of her great aunt, she was one of the beauties of this country and a very important person. One day not very long ago Madame Giroud was in the country where they all came from and she met an old woman and they talked together. Ah said the old woman Madame you do remember your great aunt. Ah yes said Madame Giroud well said the old woman, I know something about her that nobody else knows. When she was young quite young and very beautiful a soldier passed by. And your greataunt gave birth to a pair of still-born twins very little ones and she buried them under a pear tree the two of them.

Madame Giroud admitted that ever since a pear tree did give her a funny feeling.

This year as every year they gather the grapes and make the wine, they always think there will be none as in this country everything is against the wine, the late frosts, hail, mildew and not enough late sunshine, but they always have a crop all the same. This year as always they had one, quite a large one and the French like their land are economical and generous, everything has to go into it and a good deal comes out of it, and they always have to celebrate it, faire part, as it reads in their announcements of funerals wedding and births, in this country they always celebrate it by something called ramequin, it is like a welsh rarebit, only instead of beer and cheese, it is made of white wine, eggs and cheese, and everybody keeps stirring it with their very large piece of bread.

In the neighborhood here the other day they had not agreed about something so one of the neighbors was not invited. All the others were gathered together to make the ramkin, it is the only cooking any Frenchman who is a father of a family and not a professional cook ever does. The men were making the ramkin on the stove, it was a dark night, the neighbor climbed on the roof and sat on the chimney and so the smoke went back down the chimney and smoked the ramkin, the cronies thought it was the wind and began again, the man on the roof lifted himself until he heard them say now it is on and then down he sat again upon the chimney, and spoiled the ramkin, it was not until some time after that the unfortunate cooks found out why.

So the most striking thing about France is the family, and the terre, the soil of France. Revolutions come and revolutions go, fashions come and fashions go, logic and civilisation remain and with it the family and the soil of France.

They are so reasonable about that land, of course it has no value without men, and of course men cannot exist without family.

The family, any family has naturally the quality of the concentration of isolation. That is what makes a family, that is what makes war, so much war, it is that concentration of isolation. And the French who do not want war live through war calmly, because after all it is the concentration of isolation which is a family in peace as well as in war.

As a cultivated earth has nothing brutal or really cruel about it so the Frenchman is neither brutal nor cruel. They invented the word sadism but their sadism has to do with the passions and the passions have nothing to do with the earth or with the family, that is like revolutions and other things a thing apart.

One of the things that is very evident in France is that children are never punished not even much corrected. They from the beginning are French that is logical civilised and have a sense of fashion and a complete realisation of the facts of life. Any French child can thoroughly understand anything.

The one rare time I ever saw a boy crying was one day down by the quays in Paris.

The quays in Paris have never changed, that is to say they look different but the life that goes on there is always the same. It was only last year that I really got to know them, I had put my car in a garage below Notre Dame and every morning and every evening I went the length of the quays forward and back. I found that going down below near the water I could let my dogs loose because we crossed no streets and then I found that the life there below was very pleasant, it had nothing whatever to do with the life of a city, that is one of the characteristic things of the French, the city and country the country and city are not separated. Everybody in the city has relations in the country and everybody in the country has relations in the city and everybody in the city expects to return to something in the country all the employees of the state all policemen all workmen of all sorts, in fact practically everybody even the shopkeepers do expect to retire eventually to the country, that is where inevitably you live when you no longer have to work for a living, when you have a pension when you have saved some thing and you grow vegetables and you build yourself a little house and you hope that money won't change so much but that you can live on what you have. Anyway you can always have vegetables and rabbits and chickens and that is always something.

Of course money has done a lot of changing but there is always the hope that it will stay put sometime. Anyway the French people never take money very seriously, they save it certainly they horde it very carefully but they know really that it has no very great permanence. That is the reason they all want a place in the country. Lots of people we know have tried to buy a house in this neighborhood and they are always surprised that nobody wants to sell, neither the peasants or the small people or the bigger people. But as they all say if we sell our home what will we have for it, money, and what is the use of that money, money goes and after it is gone then where are we, beside we have all we want, what can we do with money except lose it, money to spend is not very welcome, if you have it and you try to spend it, well spending money is an anxiety, saving money is a comfort and a pleasure, economy is not a duty it is a comfort, avarice is an excitement, but spending money is nothing, money spent is money non-existent, money saved is money realised, even as it did the other day in the village it got burned up.

There was a fire in an isolated barn down in the valley and it was in the day-time and the locksmith who is the head of the fire-brigade was trying to put out the fire but as the barn was full of hay it was pretty hopeless.

The barn belonged to one man and the hay belonged to another man and everybody seemed rather philosophical about it all, the barn was old and it had been a good barn for hay and the owner of the hay had plenty more and then suddenly somebody remembered that there was a lean-to that belonged to still somebody else and vaguely somebody remembered that he had said once that he had left things there, so somebody went off to find the man who owned the lean-to. He was not busy but he did not want to come but finally he was induced to come and in the meanwhile they had gone into the lean-to, and there they found some clothes and some bedding and in a jug forty thousand francs.

When the owner was confronted with this he said yes, it was his pension, he was a widower, he had plenty to eat from his land, they gave him this money, he had to go in town for it but as he had no use for it he left it there in the lean-to.

What he did with it when they finally gave it to him I do not know, but I suppose he left it somewhere else.

French people do not like to spend money it worries them, they take luxuries naturally, if you have them they are not luxuries and if you do not have them they still are not luxuries.

And so on the banks of the Seine down by the water there is no city life at all, it is an easy life and each person lives it for himself.

So one day there I saw a boy about thirteen years of age a stout well-set up and comfortably dressed boy sitting by the water-side, next to him was a woman evidently not his mother but a relation and there they sat. Large tears were rolling down his cheeks. What is it, I asked her, oh she said sorrow, but it will pass. He has failed in his examinations, but it will pass. And quite impersonally she sat by and indeed it was sorrow but as she said, sorrow passes.

It is a queer life down there by the river. One day I was coming along and there were two men, one of them had found a high hat and also some orange flowers which he had pinned on the hat, and as they came along, the one presented the other to every one, he is my brother, he said of the other.

The barges always grow flowers and the men

always come down with mimosa in their hand and disappear somewhere with it, and there are cardboard beds under the bridges, cardboard apparently is good against the cold anyway they use it, and the women wash their clothes and the men fish there and artists paint there and everybody minds their own business. They talk and grumble mostly to themselves but nobody fights with anybody else.

So children are never harshly treated in France. A child in France is a thing of value, it is not a treasure but it is like anything that belongs to the earth it has a value and a valuable thing is always well taken care of, and the French use everything but they abuse nothing.

So the twentieth century did need France as a background. France might play with the idea of the destruction of the family as the beginning and end of everything but it could never really convince any Frenchman and so France was a background for the beginning of the twentieth century, it had had its one real effort to believe that the family and the things the family holds in its hands and walks on and eats and drinks and which belong to that family, they had their try-out of trying not to believe in this in the beginning of the nineteenth century in the first french revolution, but it really was not interesting.

Wars yes and excitement yes, but really not interesting. There is no logic to it, no civilisation to it and no fashion.

So when the twentieth century was going to start in to try it out all over again, the Frenchmen were very content to be in it but not of it.

In France the family life is never so much a family life as in vacation. The family is always the family but during vacations it is an extended family and that is exhausting.

A Frenchman once told me that he was haunted it was his obsession what he called vacation weather. I said it is just summer weather, no he said it has a kind of weight to it that is not summer but vacation weather.

In every country house all the in-laws come and all their children and all their servants, in-laws only visit each other in winter, they visit a great deal and they all eat together somewhere at least once a week but in the vacation they live together.

Then came the twentieth century with its automobiles particularly after the war, the French family lived less together in vacations because they naturally moved around more. They all pretty well concluded that this was even more exhausting than all living together and not as healthy for children and every one.

Getting in and out of trains was better because trains are always stopping but automobiles just kept going. Now in this new war all the country is filled with all the relations living together but it is not vacation weather, it is not even vacation so everybody is happier beside that they cannot move around even in trains so it is not so exhausting. It is a permanent residence and that changes everything. In-laws are now a permanency and so except for the very often repeated statement that some cousin is a woman really utterly wearisome, and a French family is always of the same mind, they all find the same person the most tiresome, and there are always the certain amount of trouble about mother-in-laws, and daughter-in-laws, but all this is very much softened by the son and husband being away at the war. And many financial arrangements which were inevitable because of troubles between daughter-in-laws and widowed mother-in-laws rest in abeyance. And that makes everything easier.

In France letters are not shared. Each one has their own letter. Any member of any class in France will say I have had no news but my mother has, or I have had no news but my son has. Well said I once in astonishment do they not read you what is in their letter, I was going to say do they not show you the letter but I knew instinctively that that would not do. Oh yes is the answer, he or she reads me what he or she chooses.

Everything is private and personal in France and at the same time a family is always together. Even in the midst of the war letters are not shared. As my old servant Hélène once said, no Madame it is not a secret but one does not tell it.

I really have never known Paris in the midst of a declaration of war. Wars always take place in vacation time and in vacation weather, so one is not in Paris. Paris is always there, at least we in the country suppose so although at such a time we are not very conscious of its existence, the beginning of war is so occupying where you are, that even Paris is not there. Such is the concentration of isolation which is war.

Paris is there and gradually even here quite far away one begins to know that it is there.

I have never known Paris in the beginning of a war, I have known Paris during the war not this time but the last time, this time I only knew it for half a day.

I have however known Paris since the beginning of the twentieth century until now, known it pretty well.

When I first knew Paris again since childhood in 1900 and then only on vacation France meant Paris,

France meant Paris and its immediate surroundings. The Paris which was France as I knew it then was completely republican.

I knew an American Mrs. Dawson, I met her in England and she said she had abandoned Paris after 1870. She said the manners of the French as republicans were not the delightful manners of Paris as an Empire. To be sure everybody in the republic was addressed as Monsieur and Madame. Even the butcher boy quite young would say bon-jour Madame to our servant and she would equally seriously bon-jour Monsieur to him although he was only fifteen. I do not know whether during the empire this was true. At any rate although there are always monarchists and imperialists in France, most unexpected ones sometimes, actually they in their hearts pretty much all of them are republicans and want a republic, because they know that the family is so strong in France that the hereditary principle should be kept out of the government, it just should.

Beside the republic so far has pretty well done what they all think a government should do, let them alone, protected them, on the whole, from the enemy, and though it costs a good deal, this government, it might cost more if it were another government, and no piece of it gets so well established that it can go too far in any direction. And so as governments go the third republic is not so bad. It might be worse, it might be better, but it is not too bad.

In Paris around 1900–1914 the men were elegant and had almost more beauty of elegance than the women. When we came to Paris the men wearing their silk hats on the side of their head and leaning heavily on their cane toward the other side making a balance, the heavy head the heavy hand on the cane were the elegance of Paris. The women were plain, fashionable more than elegant in contrast with the men. As the century progressed the war came. The horizon blue and the black uniforms of the aviators continued the tradition of French elegance among the men. The women for a while did lose fashion and slowly then the men lost their elegance and the women regained their fashion and then they were no longer plain they were pretty and for a while, it was another ideal. After this war the men very likely will regain elegance and the women fashion and elegance. It is all very exciting.

Flowers and fruits were very much rarer in the beginning of the century than now. In those days flowers and fruits were rare and being rare were very elegant.

They were very carefully cultivated to look well and be well in relation to the thing near which they were to be placed, either people or things, they had nothing to do with out-of-doors, they had entirely to do with indoors, and the arrangement of the fruits and flowers were traditional elegant and fashionable.

I can remember the horror of our Bretonne servant in Palma when we used to bring in armfuls of flowers and put them all over the house. Now any French person can bear flowers anywhere and in any quantity with equanimity but not then. It was also true of fruits. Fruits were a wonderful size, almost always with a design stencilled upon them when they were in the act of growing and very expensive. No one was ever allowed to touch them. There were only these very wonderful fruits and ordinary apples practically nothing else and these ordinary apples were always wormy. Since then fruits in the smallest provincial town are to be found in great abundance, everybody eats fruit and fruit is really no longer a thing to admire or to have as an adjunct to an elegant table. The same is true with flowers. Flowers are now bought in great bunches and anybody within reason can have all they want. So now flowers are almost arranged in many homes in the English manner lots of flowers everywhere and the new interest in flowers is to arrange them to give an effect of violence, of activity, of strangeness. Gradually that is producing its own elegance.

I was talking to Madame Giroud, she remembers everything and I asked her what seemed to her the most startling difference between the France of her youth the Nineteenth century and the France of to-day. She said undoubtedly the difference in dress of the people living not in cities but in the country. Not alone the girls but the women in villages and country towns all dress well, all clean themselves very much more.

I know that I was much taken with the short sleeves short dresses as being an enormous incentive to personal cleanliness. There was a very great difference between before and after the war about that. It was true of the younger women and even true of the older women.

On the other hand except the introduction of electric light the inside of the houses in the villages and in the country have not changed much. Of course the existence of electric light in itself made things different because any one can see everything more clearly. Then young men have changed and are athletic and clean but as they grow older they tend to be more as they were. The women keep up the standard and that has its great influence upon the children. The men less. I am now speaking of the country and not of the cities. One of the most important things in the city was the introduction of central heating. The houses the shops in Paris and in the other large cities suddenly became very hot. That had to do naturally with the change in fashion of the women the short sleeves the short skirts the lack of underclothes the thinness of the stockings, and as France makes the fashions for everybody the central heating created in the cities in France made the styles. The styles went with the Americanisation of Europe so pronounced immediately after the war, hygienes, bath-tubs, and sport.

Later on and until just now there have been persistent attempts to get back or forward to styles that cover more, and until now they have been resisted because the conditions that produced the post-war fashions more or less persisted. Gradually though the desire to spend money slackened, it was more difficult to make money and therefore there began a tendency to save it. In the old nineteenth century France you were always supposed to live on your last year's income never on your current income. And now every one was living in France on this year's income or next year's income, they were living on the instalment plan, in short they were not being themselves. And slowly they were beginning resenting this tendency, it came from all classes this resistance and the fashions went with it the effort to re-establish more covering to the body longer skirts more durable clothes.

Now there is war, the houses in Paris are not centrally heated any more. In many apartment houses you heat yourself as you can. Many people like ourselves are staying in the country with the boulets fire of France which I have not seen since 1900 and wood fires to help and naturally woollen stockings and other things accompany this and fashions are changing. The darkness has a great deal to do with everything. Madame Giroud always tells me you do not know what these villages were in the old days and even now although the roads are dark the houses and the barns are lighted electrically inside, all the streets are dark but the shops are bright inside. So although they look mediæval outside they do not feel mediæval inside. So even when it is black outside in the twentieth century it is brightly lighted inside. Which was not true of the nineteenth century.

The boulets fires of France the round walnuts of pressed coal that were in all houses in the beginning of the twentieth century quite entirely ceased to exist even in the country, the grates that were put in to the fireplace and balanced by a bit of brick and filled with the walnut coal that gave out a steady small heat and never really seemed to change night or day were not seen any more. And now there is 1939 and war and everybody wants their boulets fire back again. We have one. We found the grates still in the local shops with the same curly design as one we found in the garret of this house which dates from we do not know when. Those in the shops are of exactly the same design which shows how dead boulets fires had been.

And so a century is made of one hundred years and a hundred years is not so long. Anybody can know somebody who remembers somebody else and makes it go back one hundred years. If it cannot be done in two generations it can be done easily done in three. And so one hundred years is not so long.

It is rather a worry that our civilisation if you think of it in the form of three generations making a century does not take many generations to begin.

A century is one hundred years. Every century has a beginning and a middle and an ending. Every century is like the life of any one, the life of any nation, that is to say it begins that is it has a childhood it has an adolescence it has an adult life, it has a middle life an older life and then it ends.

The nineteenth century did all this, the twentieth century is doing it. I imagine any century does.

It begins as a child begins trailing its clouds of glory from the century which has just been. Of course the twentieth century did that. Only a small part of those in the commencing of the twentieth century started it as a twentieth century and not a left over nineteenth century. It began in uncertainty, it walked with difficulty, it rather just crept along.

And then slowly it went through its adolescence and then the world war came, and that made everybody know it was not the nineteenth century but the twentieth century.

I asked Madame Pierlot, she had been raised in the country, she was a provincial, she had never been to Paris, she had been the wife of a military attaché at various capitals and then just in the beginning of the century she went to Paris as a woman of forty. I said to her how did you feel about it. Well she said I was disappointed in it. But why, well she said I thought it was not as concentrated as embassadorial circles in other countries, I found French people in Paris, sophisticated and not very exciting. And then, she added, I found that Parisians were much more interesting when you had them in the country. I ceased to see them in Paris I had them come to stay with me in the country, and then I knew that Parisians were interesting.

She then went on to tell me of when she first went to Paris she went to a dinner and sat next to Anatole France. After a little while he said Madame you are not a Parisian you have always lived in the provinces. Yes she said. That he said is admirable, continue, live in Paris but always remain provincial.

And so the century only slowly began to come of age, the war was a struggle and it made the twentieth century self-conscious. Everybody in it knew the twentieth century for what it was.

France had not really been interested in the twentieth century England had refused the twentieth century, and now the world war made them both make up their minds that the twentieth century was there, it was going through the agony through which all adolescence has to go, it was suffering as all adolescents suffer and there it was it was the twentieth century.

And France and England after the war began to feel a little that the twentieth century would have to get civilised. It would have to go through that period of revolution that every young person goes through, when they think that systems will not be systems but something else, when every one is certain that they can reform everybody if they only go the right way to work at it.

This was the first war period, a period of fashion without style, of systems with disorder, of reforming everybody which is persecution, and of violence without hope. All this is natural after adolescence before the process of civilising of recognising the right of every one not to be reformed which comes when people become adult.

And now France and England are hoping to do this thing now it is almost forty years old the century and it was time it was becoming civilised time it was beginning to be grown up, time to settle down to middle age and a pleasant life and the enjoyment of ordinary living.

So this book is dedicated to France and England.

France who was the background of all who were excited and determined and created by the twentieth century but who herself was not at the time enormously interested. France really prefers civilisation to tumultuous adolescence, France prefers that the adolescent learns reserve and logic and civilisation and fashion as he emerges out of adolescence, France who thinks that childhood and adolescence should be felt instinctively as not an end in itself but as a progression toward the state of being civilised. And England who like a boy who has not gone to school because his people did not believe in any of the schools that were then existing and who then considerably older does go to school and very quickly catches up and passes the others who have been at school from the beginning because England did refuse the twentieth century, did not believe it was really there thought everybody had made a mistake except themselves, they who knew it was still the nineteenth century.

And now they know.

This book is dedicated to France and England who are to do what is the necessary thing to do, they are going to civilise the twentieth century and make it be a time when anybody can be free, free to be civilised and to be.

The century is now forty years old, too old to do what it is told.

It is old enough to like to live quietly and well, to go to heaven or to hell as they like, to know that to live as they please is pleasanter than to be told.

So this is what England and France are going to do and this book is dedicated to them because I want them to do what they are going to do. Thank you.

SIR FRANCIS ROSE   *Gertrude Stein at Bilignin*